Transition Tips and Tricks
for Teachers

This book is dedicated to my aunts,

Mary McCracken and Elizabeth Zimmerman,

who added a little magic to my childhood.

from the author of Transition Time

transition tips and tricks

For Teachers

Prepare young children for changes in the day and focus their attention with these smooth, fun, and meaningful transitions!

Jean Feldman

Illustrations K. Whelan Dery

gryphon house®, inc.

Beltsville, Maryland

Acknowledgments

Special thanks to Kathy Charner, who is the best editor and magician of all!

She can take my ideas and scribbles and turn them into a wonderful book for teachers.

Thanks to all the teachers who so generously shared their ideas and

"tricks" with me so that I could pass them on to you.

Thanks to the children whose smiles, laughter, and twinkling eyes continue to verify

that the activities in this book do work.

And thanks to my family who humors me, supports me,

and is, indeed, the wind beneath my wings!

Gryphon House books are available at special discount when purchased in bulk for special premiums and sales promotions as well as for fund-raising use. Special editions or book excerpts also can be created to specification. For details, contact the Director of Marketing at the address below.

Gryphon House, Inc., 10726 Tucker Street, Beltsville MD, 20705 or P.O. Box, Beltsville MD 20705-0207.

   Library of Congress Cataloging-in-Publication Data
Feldman, Jean R., 1947-
    Transition tips and tricks for teachers: prepare young children for changes in the day and focus their attention with these smooth, fun, and meaningful transitions! / Jean Feldman; illustrations by K. Whelan Dery.
       p. cm.
    Includes bibliographical references and index.
    ISBN 0-87659-216-7
    1. Early childhood education—Activity programs. 2. Early childhood teachers. I. Title.

LB1139.35.A37 F48 2000
372.13—dc21

                                                                    00-035368

Table of Contents

Chapter 4—Attention Grabbers, Puppets, and Finger Fun 67

Chapter 5—Great Ideas for Rainy Days (or any day) 83

Chapter 6—Sing, Rhyme, and Chant! 105

Songs

Chapter 7—A Story for Your Pocket . .143

Chapter 8—Tricks for Any Time! 167

Introduction

Tune Into Children and Tune Into Learning!

Teaching and guiding children through daily transitions requires a little magic, and this book is full of special tricks for you! With these activities your day will move more smoothly, behavior problems will decrease, and you will be stimulating children's brains. Above all, children will be delighted with the songs, puppets, props, stories, and games.

Brain research provides insight to help us "tune into" children and how they learn. This book integrates brain research with practical classroom experience. Not surprisingly, the applications brain experts suggest are the very ones loving, child-centered teachers and parents have used for centuries!

Underlying brain research principles reflected in this book include:

The brain loves novelty. The best way to get children's attention and interest is to surprise them with something new!

The brain likes to be challenged. Children are naturally curious and interested in the world around them. The brain enjoys thinking—that's what it was designed to do! We can enhance thinking by asking open-ended questions.

Sensory stimulation is essential to learning. The best way for information to reach the brain is through the senses. The more senses involved in an activity, the more likely it is that learning will occur.

Feedback is critical to learning. The more immediate the feedback, the more likely that permanent learning will occur.

Children thrive in a safe, secure environment. If children feel threatened or are stressed, they will not achieve optimal development.

The brain responds positively to schedules, routines, and rituals. Schedules and routines help children know what to expect. Daily rituals, such as greetings and songs, "jump start" the brain and act like "indicators" to elicit desired behaviors.

Children need caring, consistent relationships and positive role models. Because children learn more from our actions than our words, we should model the behavior we expect from them.

Emotional factors are important to learning. Children need to feel good about themselves and positive about school. Community celebrations and group activities can help foster these attitudes.

The brain needs healthy foods, rest, and water. Children need healthy snacks and meals for mental as well as physical growth. Rest gives the brain time to process information. Water is also needed frequently to rehydrate the brain.

Timing must be considered. The brain thrives on a balance of active and quiet periods. Children need "brain breaks" when they get up, move around, and get oxygen going to the brain.

The classroom environment has an impact on learning. So many factors in the classroom can enhance or detract from learning. For example, the brain likes natural sunlight, fresh air, and cool temperatures. It also likes plants and softness. Choose neutral background colors, so children and their work receive the most attention. Aromas, such as peppermint and citrus, can stimulate children's brains, while lavender tends to calm behavior. Seating arrangements can also affect learning. Having children work in a circle or small groups facing each other encourages group cohesiveness.

Level of interest and play are of utmost consideration. Children are more likely to learn if it's fun and interesting to them.

The brain learns through integration and association. Learning should be integrated and should occur within the context of daily experiences. Children need to associate new learning with previous experiences. Facts learned in isolation are soon forgotten!

Language is essential to learning. Children need to talk about their experiences to "own" them.

Laughter is good for the brain. A good laugh gets oxygen going to the brain and relieves stress.

Stories are a powerful way to store experiences in the brain. Read and tell stories frequently to children, and involve them in acting out stories.

The brain loves music and rhythm. Music, music, music! Music can be used to enhance learning, and songs and chants are a convenient way for the brain to "store" information.

Movement stimulates the brain. Running, jumping, marching, skipping, twirling, galloping, and swinging all exercise the brain.

Crossover movements "unstick" the brain. There is a line down the middle of the body called the midline. Whenever you engage children in cross-lateral activities, it wakes up the brain.

Small motor activities stimulate the brain. When children do fingerplays, work puzzles, or play with playdough, they are using their brains.

Repetition is critical to permanent learning. Children must do activities over and over again. Listen when they beg you to repeat songs, stories, and games they enjoy!

Resources and References

Armstrong, Thomas. 1993. *Seven Kinds of Smart: Identifying and Developing Your Many Intelligences*. Alexandria, VA: Association for Supervision and Curriculum Development.

Caine, Renata, and Geoffrey Caine. 1994. *Making Connections: Teaching the Human Brain*. Boston: Addison-Wesley.

Gardner, Howard. 1991. *The Unschooled Mind: How Children Learn and How Schools Should Teach*. New York: Basic Books.

Healy, Jane. 1990. *Endangered Minds: Why Our Children Can't Think*. New York: Simon and Schuster.

Jensen, Eric. 1996. *Brain Based Learning*. Del Mar, CA: Turning Point Publishing.

Jensen, Eric. 1997. *Brain Compatible Strategies*. Del Mar, CA: Turning Point Publishing.

Schiller, Pam. 1999. *Start Smart! Building Brain Power in the Early Years*. Beltsville, MD: Gryphon House.

Shore, Rima. 1997. *Rethinking the Brain: New Insights Into Early Development*. New York: Families and Work Institute.

Wolfe, Pat. 1996. *Mind, Memory, and Learning: Translating Brain Research to Classroom Practice*. Front Royal, VA: National Cassette Services.

The brain is always looking for patterns. Patterns help us make connections, file new information, and predict what will happen next.

Recall can enhance learning. Give children opportunities to review what they have learned and to summarize their experiences.

Above all, remember each child's brain is unique and different. One size does not fit all; therefore, we must incorporate a variety of instructional strategies into our programs.

The goal of this book is to provide you with techniques and materials that can help you exercise children's brains by integrating the above principles. I often tell teachers, "If you're not having fun, you're doing something wrong!" Childhood is so precious and fleeting; we have a responsibility to make it as rich and wonderful as possible. My wish is that this book will add some fun, excitement, and meaningful learning experiences, and create magical childhood memories for children!

CHAPTER 1
Starting the Day

Begin with these activities to "jump start" the brain

and prepare children for a great day!

Mozart-Food for the Brain!

Play Mozart as the children arrive in the morning, just before circle time, or any time during the day to create a positive learning environment.

WHAT?

Mozart recording

tape or CD player

HOW?

- Play the music softly in the background as children come into the classroom.

- At circle time, ask them if they noticed anything different when they came in the room. Have they ever heard music like that before?

- Tell them that the music was written by Mozart and that you've read that classical music by Mozart and others can help their brains work better.

- Continue playing classical music each day as children arrive at school.

HINT!
Your local public library has a wide selection of classical music and many other types of recordings.

WHAT ELSE?
Experiment with other types of music. What happens if you play jazz, country, ragtime, or ethnic music as children arrive at school? Does it influence their behavior?

Ask children to comment on how various types of music makes them feel.

Use background music during rest time, independent reading time, or other times during the day, and notice the effect on children.

Greeter

Start the day right by making each child feel special with this routine.

HOW?

- Stand at the door as school begins and say to each child, "I'm so glad to see you," or "I've been waiting for you."

- Give them a pat on the back, hug, or handshake as they enter the room.

- Add the following chant to this routine.

  Hello!

  Hello! Good day!
  You're looking mighty fine.
  Come on in,
  And have a good time.

  Hello, (child's name).
  You're looking mighty fine.
  Come on in,
  And have a good time.

WHAT?

no materials needed

WHAT ELSE?

After you have modeled this, choose a child to be the "greeter." This could become a regular classroom job or a task for the children who arrive early.

Make a badge for the greeter, or give her a special hat to wear.

Sign-In Poster

Children sign their names or make their "marks" as they enter the classroom each day.

WHAT?

poster board

erasable markers

laminating machine
or clear contact paper

string or yarn

tape

HOW?

• Print "Sign In, Please" at the top of the poster board.

• Laminate it or cover with clear contact paper. Hang it on the classroom door.

• Tie a piece of string or yarn to an erasable marker and tape it to the side of the poster as shown.

• Explain to the children how much it means to you to have each of them at school every day.

• To help you know they are present, ask them to sign the poster on the door before they come in the room. Each child can write her name, make a mark, or draw a little picture.

Sign in, Please

tom

🐱 kitty

GAbe

WHAT ELSE?

Tape a class roster beside the sign-in poster to provide children with a model for writing their names.

Use the poster at circle time to take attendance. Instead of writing their names, ask children to draw a face that represents how they are feeling.

Use a dry erase board or chalkboard instead of the poster board and markers.

HINT!

Choose one child each day to be your helper and erase the poster at the end of the day.

Morning Matchup

This activity nurtures children's reading skills as they arrive at school.

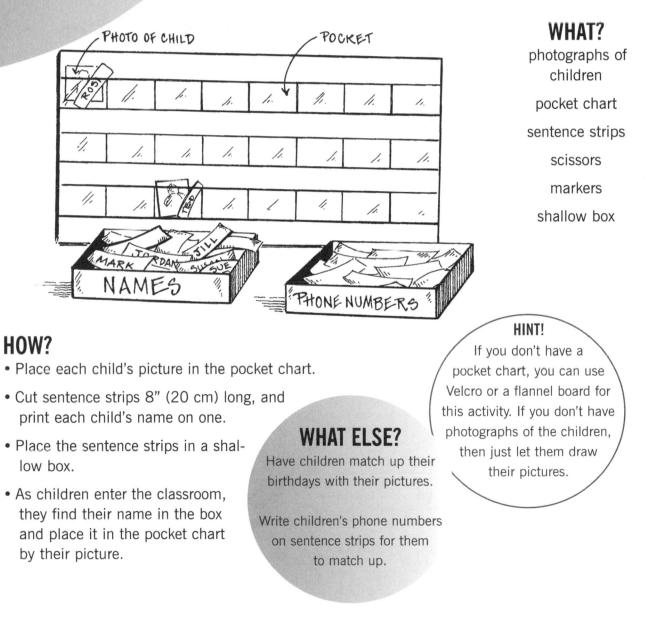

PHOTO OF CHILD — POCKET

NAMES

PHONE NUMBERS

WHAT?

photographs of children

pocket chart

sentence strips

scissors

markers

shallow box

HOW?

- Place each child's picture in the pocket chart.

- Cut sentence strips 8" (20 cm) long, and print each child's name on one.

- Place the sentence strips in a shallow box.

- As children enter the classroom, they find their name in the box and place it in the pocket chart by their picture.

WHAT ELSE?

Have children match up their birthdays with their pictures.

Write children's phone numbers on sentence strips for them to match up.

HINT!

If you don't have a pocket chart, you can use Velcro or a flannel board for this activity. If you don't have photographs of the children, then just let them draw their pictures.

Hugs, Smiles, Shakes, and High Fives

This morning ritual recognizes that children have different feelings. It gives them the opportunity to express their needs and start the day in a personal way.

WHAT?

felt scraps

scissors

HOW?

• Cut a heart, lips, hand, and the numeral five out of felt using the patterns on page 19. Enlarge patterns as needed.

• Place the shapes on the floor, and explain what each symbol represents.

  Heart—Give me a hug.
  Lips—Give me a smile.
  Hand—Give me a handshake.
  Five—Give me a "high five."

• Children stand on a symbol, then you give them the greeting they request.

WHAT ELSE?

At circle time, have children greet each other with hugs, smiles, handshakes, or high fives. Talk about how people in different countries greet each other or say good morning.

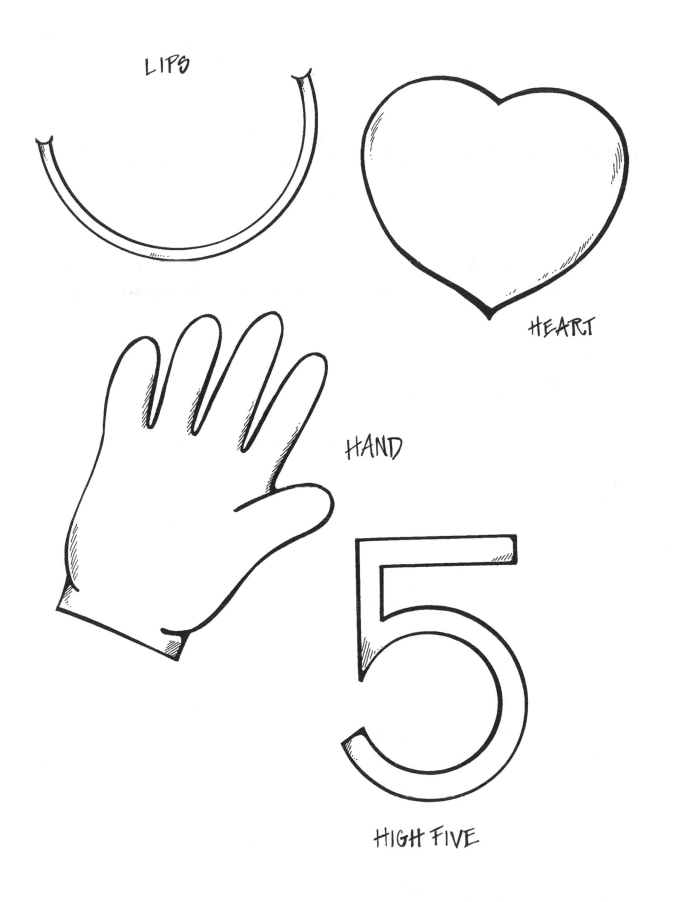

LIPS

HEART

HAND

HIGH FIVE

Hello, Neighbor!

Brain research emphasizes the importance of using rituals and songs to start each day. This partner game will also build community and create positive feelings.

WHAT?

no materials needed

HOW?

• Demonstrate the chant and movements with a partner.

• Each child gets a partner and slowly repeats the chant and actions.

• Continue chanting the poem, changing partners each time after you turn around.

Hello, Neighbor!

Hello, neighbor. (wave to partner)
What do you say? (give high five)
It's going to be a happy day. (clap hands)
Greet your neighbor. (shake hands)
Boogie on down. (wiggle hips)
Give a bump, (gently bump hips)
And turn around. (turn around, then move to a new partner)

• Try singing the poem to the tune of "Good Night, Ladies."

WHAT ELSE?

Write the words to this song on a chart. Encourage the children to "read" the words as you point to them.

Begin the song with two children doing the dance while the other children sit on the floor. After chanting one verse, they each select a new partner. After the second round, the four children standing each select a new partner. The chant continues until every child is standing and participating.

Everybody Shake a Hand

Here's a happy tune to start your day and create group cohesiveness.

HOW?

• Begin singing the song and modeling what the children are to do:

**Everybody Shake a Hand
(Tune: "Buffalo Gal")**

*Everybody shake a hand, (shake children's hands as you walk around the room)
Shake a hand,
Shake a hand.
Everybody shake a hand,
And walk around the room.*

Everybody give high five... (slap right hands together in the air)

Everybody scratch a back... (scratch each other's backs)

*Everybody give a hug, (end by giving hugs, then sitting down)
Give a hug,
Give a hug.
Everybody give a hug,
And then you take a seat.*

WHAT?

no materials needed

WHAT ELSE?

Ask the children to suggest verses for different things they could do, such as "bow to a friend," "give a smile," "say hello," "give a bump," etc.

I Like You!

Use this tune to start your day, focus children's attention for a story, or throughout the day to prepare children for transitions.

WHAT?

no materials needed

HOW?

Sing the following, pointing to a different child each time.

I Like You (Tune: "Flies in the Buttermilk")
I like you, (point to self, then a child)
There's no doubt about it. (shake head, "no")
I like you, (point to self, then a child)
There's no doubt about it. (shake head)
I like you, (point to self, then a child)
There's no doubt about it. (shake head)
You are my good friend. (point to children and look them in the eyes)
You like me, (point to child, then self)
There's no doubt about it. (shake head)
You like me, (point to child, then self)
There's no doubt about it. (shake head)
You like me, (point to child, then self)
There's no doubt about it, (shake head)
You are my good friend. (point to children)

WHAT ELSE?

Discuss what it means to be a friend. Ask children to draw pictures and dictate sentences about friendship. Put their pages together to make a book called, "How to Be a Friend."

Secret Password

The Secret Password is a clever way to repeat key information.

HOW?

- Write a letter, shape, color, word, or other piece of information on the paper. (Relate this to skills you are working on, and change it as needed.)

- Tape the paper over the door.

- Explain to the children that you will have a Secret Password above the door each day when they arrive. They have to whisper the password to you before they can come in the room.

- When the children first come into the room, be available to help them identify the password. Give them hints if they have difficulty, and provide them with immediate feedback.

WHAT?

paper

markers

tape

circle

PAPER TAPED TO DOOR WAY

WHAT ELSE?

You can use this technique first thing in the morning, or use it throughout the day and have the children repeat it to you each time they enter the classroom.

Reinforce the password by putting it on the screen saver on your classroom computer.

Brain Sprinkles

Jump start children's brains each day with "brain sprinkles."

WHAT?

plastic can or jar with a lid

contact paper

markers

¼ cup (50 ml) rice

glue

HOW?

• Cover the can with contact paper. Decorate with markers and write "Brain Sprinkles" on the can.

• Put ¼ cup (50 ml) rice in the can and glue or tape on the lid.

• To start the day, tell the children you're going to give them some "brain sprinkles" that will help them think better.

• Walk around the room and gently shake the can over each child's head.

• At the conclusion of a learning experience or at the end of the day, ask them how the "brain sprinkles" worked. What did they learn?

PLASTIC JAR

¼ CUP RICE

CONTACT PAPER

LID

WHAT ELSE?

Label cans "quiet sprinkles" or "dream sprinkles," and use them throughout the day to prepare children for different activities. For example, before taking them in the hall, shake "quiet sprinkles" on the children, at rest time shake "dream sprin-kles," and so on.

FINISHED PRODUCT

CHAPTER 2
Group or Circle Time

The rituals, songs, and props suggested in this chapter will turn group or circle time into a magical time and nurture group cohesiveness.

Hand Hug

A Hand Hug is a good activity to use to quiet children for a group experience.

WHAT?

no materials needed

HOW?

- Demonstrate how to give a Hand Hug by gently squeezing hands with a partner.

- Ask the children to hold hands.

- Give a Hand Hug (squeeze) to the child on your right and sit down.

- That first child squeezes the hand of the person on his right and sits down.

- The second child squeezes the hand of the person on his right and then sits down.

- The children pass the Hand Hug around the circle until everyone is seated quietly.

WHAT ELSE?

Prepare children for other activities in the day by having them do the "wave." The first child stands up, lifts his hands in the air, and sits down as the second child stands up and waves his hands in the air. Continue moving around the circle until everyone has had a turn and is focused for the next event.

I Like to Come to School

Sing this song at group or circle time to prepare children for the different activities you will do during the day.

HOW?

- Sit on the floor and begin singing the first verse to let the children know you are ready for them to join you.

    I Like to Come to School (Tune: "The Farmer in the Dell")
    I like to come to school.
    I like to come it school.
    It's fun to play and learn each day.
    I like to come to school.

- Ask the children what they are looking forward to doing at school, then insert the words in the song. For example:

    I like to (work puzzles).
    I like to (work puzzles).
    It's fun to play and learn each day.
    I like to (work puzzles).

- Continue having children tell what they want to do as you sing the words in the song.

WHAT?

no materials needed

WHAT ELSE?

Write the words as the children dictate them on a language experience chart or a dry erase board.
Use the song at the end of the school day to review all the activities you have done.

Make a class book called "I Like to Come to School."

Have all of the children draw pictures and dictate sentences about what they enjoy at school.

Choo Choo

The children will enjoy hearing their names and making the crossover motions if you sing this song to call them for a group time.

WHAT?
no materials needed

HOW?

• Extend your left arm. Take the index finger and middle finger of your right hand and move them to the beat up your left arm from the hand to the shoulder and then back down.

Choo Choo (Tune: "A Tisket, a Tasket")

Chorus
Choo choo choo choo (move fingers slowly up arm)
Choo choo choo,
Up the railroad track.
Choo choo choo choo (move fingers back down arm)
Choo choo choo,
And then it comes right back.

First it goes to (first child's name), (point to children and look them in their eyes)
Then it goes to (second child's name),
Then it goes to (third child's name),
Then it goes to (fourth child's name).
Chorus

• Continue singing each child's name in the song. By the time you finish, the whole group will have joined you and will be sitting quietly.

Stop and Drop

Try this little movement song to gather children for group or circle time and get them seated on the floor.

HOW?

• Demonstrate the motions as you sing:

Stop and Drop (Tune: "Frere Jacques")
Running, running, (run in place)
Running, running,
Hop, hop, hop, (hop on right foot)
Hop, hop, hop. (hop on left)
Tiptoe, tiptoe, (tiptoe)
Tiptoe, tiptoe.
Then I stop, (hold up hand)
And I drop! (sit down on floor)

WHAT?

no materials needed

WHAT ELSE?

Change the words of the song so children have to listen and move accordingly. You might ask them to jump, fly, swim, clap, etc. Always end with, "Then I stop, and I drop."

WIGGLE   STOP   WOBBLE

Wiggle Wobble

Use this chant to release wiggles and focus children's attention before group or circle time.

WHAT?

no materials needed

WHAT ELSE?

Let children suggest other parts of the body they can wiggle.

HOW?

• Start saying this chant and modeling what you want children to do.

• When they have joined you and are following along, move into your story or group time.

Wiggle Wobble

Heads go wiggle, wobble, (wiggle head from side to side)
Wiggle, wobble,
Wiggle, wobble.
Heads go wiggle, wobble,
Then they STOP! (freeze)

Fingers go wiggle, wobble, (wiggle fingers)
Wiggle, wobble,
Wiggle, wobble.
Fingers go wiggle, wobble,
Then they STOP! (freeze with hands in lap)

• Continue using other body parts in the poem as you wiggle them and then "freeze."

Teddy Bear

Have children act out this poem to release wiggles and prepare them for group or circle time.

HOW?

• Act out the poem below:

Teddy Bear

Teddy bear, teddy bear,
Turn around. (turn around)
Teddy bear, teddy bear,
Touch the ground. (touch ground)
Teddy bear, teddy bear,
Read the news. (pretend the read the paper)
Teddy bear, teddy bear,
Tie your shoes. (point to shoes)
Teddy bear, teddy bear,
Go upstairs. (pretend to go upstairs)
Teddy bear, teddy bear,
Say your prayers. (fold hands)
Teddy bear, teddy bear,
Turn off the lights.
Teddy bear, teddy bear,
Say good night! (pretend to sleep)

• Encourage children to pretend to be the teddy bear as you say the poem.

• At the end, they can fold their hands and pretend to go to sleep.

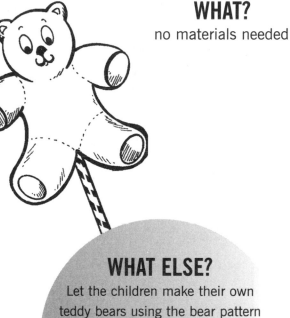

WHAT?

no materials needed

WHAT ELSE?

Let the children make their own teddy bears using the bear pattern on page 32. Tape the bear to a straw and use it to act out the poem. Challenge the children to dress their bears in different ways and to think of a name for their bears.

Sitter Spots

If children have difficulty staying in their "space" during circle time without crowding or pushing friends, Sitter Spots may be the trick for you!

HOW?

- Cut 8" (20 cm) circles from the felt to make Sitter Spots. (You will need one for each child.) Place the circles in a box or basket.

- Before a story or a group activity, have each child select a Sitter Spot.

- Tell the children to place their spots on the floor without touching anyone else's spot. (Demonstrate how to extend your arms to make sure you are not touching anyone else.)

- Explain that these are magic spots for them to sit on so they can have their own special space.

- After your group activity, have children pick up their spots and put them back in the basket.

WHAT?

felt

scissors

box or basket

WHAT ELSE?

Write children's names on the felt circles to encourage name recognition. Place the spots on the floor, then ask children to find their spots.

Let each child decorate a felt circle with markers.

Make larger "magic carpets" from felt for children to use when they read with a friend, play a game, or do other partner activities.

Carpet samples, old placemats, or laminated construction paper can also be used to help children identify their spaces.

8 CIRCLE

FELT

DECORATED SPOT WITH NAME

Ted

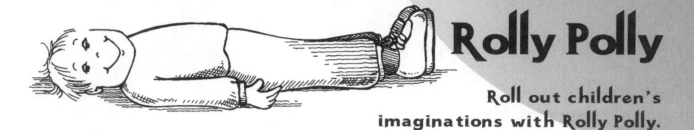

Rolly Polly

Roll out children's imaginations with Rolly Polly.

WHAT?

no materials needed

HOW?

• Ask children to extend their arms and make a large circle before sitting on the floor.

• One child at a time lies down in the center of the circle with his hands by his side like a "log."

• Place your hands gently on him as you repeat this chant:

Rolly Polly
Rolly polly, pickety pack, (pretend to roll child)
   Go see what you can see. (child rolls forward several times)
Rolly polly, pickety pack,
And then roll back to me. (child rolls back to you)

• Ask the child what he saw. Encourage him to use his imagination.

• Continue giving children a turn to roll, and then let them tell everyone what they saw.

WHAT ELSE?

Use this activity as a time to discuss "real" and "pretend." Have children determine if what their friends see is "real" or "pretend."

This is also fun to do outside on a grassy surface on a beautiful day.

Surprise Sack

This song and prop can be used at circle time or with a small group to create interest in a concept, lesson, or story.

HOW?

- Place the prop you want to use for circle time (or any surprise time) in the bag before children arrive at school.

- When they are settled for circle time, show them the bag and sing this song.

Surprise Sack (Tune: "I'm a Little Teapot")
What's in the surprise sack,
Who can tell?
Maybe it's a book, or maybe it's a shell?
What's in the surprise sack,
Who can see?
It's something special for you and me!

- Have children guess what they think is in the sack. Give them hints, then remove the object and begin your lesson.

WHAT?

paper sack or gift bag

book, item from nature, or any small object

SACK

MARBLE

COOKIE CUTTER

CRAYON

STARFISH

HINT!
Children think concretely, so show them actual examples whenever possible. Place the objects you use in the surprise sack on a special table or shelf in the classroom so children can explore them independently.

WHAT ELSE?
Spray paint a shoe box with gold paint and decorate with glitter. Change the words in the song to "surprise box."

Play "20 Questions" using the sack. Children may ask 20 "yes" or "no" questions to determine what the mystery object is.

Use a pillowcase, hip pack, purse, lunch box, or backpack to hide props that will spark children's curiosity.

Anticipation Window

Engage children's attention and reinforce visual skills with anticipation windows.

WHAT?

picture that relates to a class theme or concept

glue

file folder

scissors

HOW?

• Glue the picture to the inside of the file folder.

• Cut several three-sided slits on the front cover, as shown.

• Tell the children that you have a mystery picture inside the file folder. Explain that you'll open the windows one at a time as they try to guess what it is.

• Open the slits, encouraging the children to predict what it is. Give them hints until they have identified the picture.

• Use the picture to initiate a discussion on the topic. Questions you might ask are: "What do you think the people are saying?" "What do you think will happen next?" "How do you think they feel?"

WHAT ELSE?

Close the file folder and have children recall details from the picture.

Use book jackets in the file folder to increase interest in a book you are going to read to the class.

Use children's drawings or photographs to make anticipation windows.

FILE FOLDER

MAGAZINE PICTURE

SECTION CLOSED

SECTION OPEN

Question of the Day

The brain loves to think! We can stimulate children's thinking by asking them open-ended questions each day. Avoid judging children's answers, and encourage their creativity.

HOW?

- At circle time each day, prepare a different question for the children to answer (see examples below).

- Ask them to show you where their brain is. Explain that the brain is like the rest of the body: It loves to exercise. And the best way to exercise their brains is to think.

- Ask them to pretend to turn on their brains, then ask them the "Question of the Day." Relate the question to current events, class themes, seasonal changes, personal events, or topics that might spark their interest and curiosity.

- Here are some key words to improve questioning strategies:

  Why do you think that _____?
  I wonder what would happen if _____?
  What would you do if _____?
  How are _____ and _____ alike?
  How are _____ and _____ different?

- Rather than telling children their answers are "right" or "wrong," say "good thinking," or "that's an interesting point of view." Repeat questions and elicit other responses with, "Who else _____?" or "Does everyone agree?"

WHAT?

no materials needed

WHAT ELSE?

Write "Question of the Day" on a language experience chart or dry erase board before circle time.

Encourage children to suggest a "Question of the Day."

How are blocks
and
crayons alike?

News Time

News Time gives children the opportunity to develop language skills and will give you insight on their feelings and what's going on outside of school.

WHAT?

no materials needed

HOW?

• Begin each circle time with News Time. Go around the room, encouraging each child to share some "news" with their classmates.

HINT!

For children who tend to ramble, remind them to think of just one thing they want to say!

If children speak too softly, ask them to "turn up the volume" in their voice box.

WHAT ELSE?

Divide children into partners or small groups to share news.

Have children draw pictures of their news.

Have a sign-in board for children to write their names if they have something to share at News Time.

Use an old microphone or similar prop to pass around the room as children talk.

What's Your Bag?

Use this idea to encourage children to share about themselves, rather than bring toys for show and tell.

HOW?

- Give each child a lunch sack to decorate with his name and drawings.

- Tell children to take their bags home and bring back an object from nature the following day.

- On the next day, let children show their objects and tell one special thing they like about them.

- Label the objects and put them in the science area or on a bulletin board.

WHAT?

paper lunch sacks

markers, crayons

SACK

BASEBALL

LEAF

WHAT ELSE?

Save the bags and use them each week for a sharing activity. Here are some additional ideas for objects they could bring in:

Something in your favorite color
Wrapper from a favorite snack food
Title of a book you like
Something that you had when you were a baby
A picture of your family
Something you made
A picture of what you want to be when you grow up
A photograph of a family celebration
Words to your favorite song

PRETZEL

FAMILY PHOTO

SNAIL SHELL

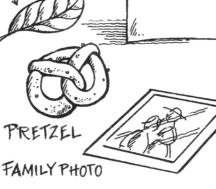

HINT!

This is a great activity for the beginning of the school year. For younger children, write a note about what they should bring in each week and put it in the bag.

Teacher of the Day

Let children take turns leading the morning routine. This will nurture their self-confidence, as well as develop their oral language.

WHAT?

cloth glove

red marker

cotton or polyester stuffing

paint stick

pipe cleaner

glue or glue gun

HOW?

- Color fingernails on the glove, as shown.

- Stuff the glove with cotton or polyester filling.

- Attach the glove to the paint stick with a pipe cleaner. Secure with glue.

- Glue down three fingers and the thumb, as shown.

- Model how to use the pointer to track a line of print, point to the date on the calendar, count the children present, etc.

- After you have modeled how to use the pointer for several weeks during circle time, choose a different child each day to hold the "official pointer" and lead the class in the morning routine.

WHAT ELSE?

Have children use the pointer to "tap" friends on the shoulder to dismiss them to a new activity or to line up.

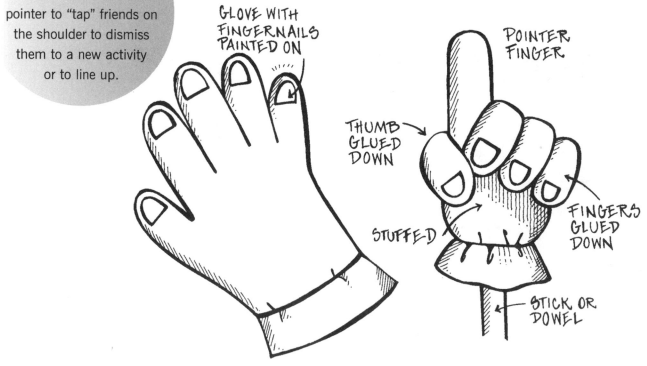

GLOVE WITH FINGERNAILS PAINTED ON

POINTER FINGER

THUMB GLUED DOWN

FINGERS GLUED DOWN

STUFFED

STICK OR DOWEL

Concept Song

Use this song at group or circle time to reinforce concepts the children are learning.

HOW?

- Sing the song below, inserting colors, shapes, letters, or words you want to review with the children:

    Concept Song (Tune: "Muffin Man")
    Do you see the (circle shape)
    The (circle shape), the (circle shape)?
    Do you see the (circle shape)
    Somewhere in the room?

- Choose a child to get up and touch something that shape.

    Yes, we see the (circle shape),
    The (circle shape), the (circle shape).
    Yes, we see the (circle shape)
    Somewhere in the room.

WHAT?

no materials needed

WHAT ELSE?

Insert colors ("Do you see the color green?"), numbers ("Do you see the number six?"), letters ("Do you see the letter 'M'?"), words ("Do you see the word 'Monday'?"), and other concepts in the song.

Use a pointer (see page 40) or magic wand (see page 159) as a prop for children to use.

Flip Your Lid!

This is a fun little review game to use with a large group or a small group. It provides immediate feedback and repetition of important skills.

WHAT?

plastic lids

stickers

WHAT ELSE?

Reinforce other concepts and categories with this game. For example, you could tell children to Flip Their Lids when you point to a circle; Flip Their Lids when you name something that is living; Flip Their Lids when you point to an object that is blue, and so on.

HOW?

• Give each child a plastic lid.

• Let them choose a sticker to go on the bottom of their lids.

• Sit in a circle with the lids on the floor in front of the children.

• Tell them that you are going to say two words. If the words rhyme, they should "flip their lids." (Demonstrate how to do this by holding up the lid so you can see the sticker.)

• If the words don't rhyme, they should leave their lids on the floor.

• Begin saying pairs of words, some that rhyme and others that do not. Children will be able to see what their friends are doing and "catch on" to rhyming words.

PLASTIC LIDS

STICKERS

Firecracker Boom!

Play this game at group or circle time to provide children with the opportunity to develop skills and concepts.

HOW?

- Choose a concept or theme that you are working on, such as letters, numerals, shapes, or sight words.

- Write the information on the index cards, and place the cards face down in the shoebox. (Make sure to make as many cards as there are children in your class.)

- Draw firecrackers similar to the one shown on three additional cards and put them in the box. Shake up the box.

- Sit in a circle and begin passing around the box.

- Each child will draw a card and identify the information on it. (If they don't know what it is, have the group help them.)

- When a child draws a card with the firecracker, they say, "Blast off!" and everyone jumps up and claps their hands over their heads as they say, "Boom!"

- The game continues until everyone has had a turn. Collect the cards, shuffle them, and play again!

WHAT?

index cards

markers

shoebox

WHAT ELSE?

Make new versions of this game to reflect different skills that need to be reinforced.

Birthday Song

Birthdays are an exciting time for children. These songs help recognize their special day.

WHAT?

no materials needed

HOW?

• When a child has a birthday, sing one of the songs below:

Today Is the Birthday (Tune: "On Top of Old Smoky")

Today is the birthday of somebody who
Is happy and smiling and right in this room.
So look all around you and tell me just who,
Is happy and smiling?
My goodness, it's YOU! (everyone points to the birthday child)

WHAT ELSE?

Mark children's birthdays on a school calendar so they can anticipate the day.

Write the words to the traditional birthday song on sentence strips. Cut between the words. The birthday child gets to mix up the words in a pocket chart and challenge his friends to sing the "jumbled up" version.

Birthday Cadence (Children repeat each line.)

I don't know but I've been told. (alternate slapping thighs to the beat)
Someone here is getting old.
It is someone's special day.
This is what we want to say.
Happy.
Birthday.
Happy birthday—to you!
(say this line together)

HINT!

If children have birthdays in the summer or during school vacations, make sure to have a "pretend" birthday for them.

A Special Birthday Cake

Here's another unique idea for celebrating birthdays that doesn't cost a thing!

HOW?

- When a child has a birthday, have the class form a giant birthday cake by holding hands and standing in a circle.

- The birthday child gets in the middle and selects friends to be the "candles" on his cake. If the child is five, he selects five friends; if he is six, he selects six friends, and so on.

- The "candles" put their hands over their heads to make a flame. After singing the birthday song, the birthday child goes up to each candle and pretends to blow it out.

- The candles slither to the ground one at a time.

- End by asking the birthday child to make a special wish.

WHAT?

no materials needed

WHAT ELSE?

Do this birthday fingerplay:

Today is (child's name) birthday,
So let's make a cake.
Mix it, then into the oven to bake. (pretend to stir)
Frost it with icing so sugary sweet. (frost cake)
And sprinkles to make it a special treat. (add sprinkles)
Stick in (age of child) candles (pretend to put in candles and light)
That we will light.
To make (child's name) birthday
Happy and bright.
Now, take a big breath, (breathe deep)
And make a wish, too. (close eyes)
Then blow them all out. (blow!)
Happy Birthday to you!
(point to birthday child)

Birthday Bag

Make this bag for children to take home to celebrate their special day.

WHAT?

backpack, cloth bag, or lunch box

book about a birthday, paper hat, small gift, or concentration game made out of birthday stickers, birthday cards

spiral notebook

crayons

HOW?

• Fill the backpack, cloth bag, or lunch box with the items suggested or other goodies.

• The birthday child gets to take the bag home on his special day.

• The child also gets to draw a picture about his birthday and dictate a story about it in the spiral notebook.

• Read the story when the child returns the bag the following day.

WHAT ELSE?

Create a "birthday card" center so classmates can make cards for their "birthday friends." You might fill a tub with construction paper, tape, ribbon, wrapping paper, scissors, envelopes, stickers, markers, etc.

Make a "birthday vest" from a large paper grocery sack for the birthday child. Let all the children in the class sign their names and decorate it with pictures as they arrive at school; then present it to the birthday child at circle time.

Roll and Review

Use an old beach ball in this enjoyable way to reinforce skills.

HOW?

- Sit in a circle on the floor and play one (or more) of the following games:

- Rhyme Ball–Say a word, then roll the ball to a child. The child says a word that rhymes, then rolls the ball back to the teacher.

- Letter Ball–Write letters on the ball with a permanent marker. When the teacher rolls the ball to a child, he must identify the letter on top or think of a word that begins with that sound before rolling the ball to another friend.

- Numeral Ball–Write numerals on the ball, then have children identify the numeral on top as they catch the ball.

WHAT?

beach ball or other large playground ball

permanent marker

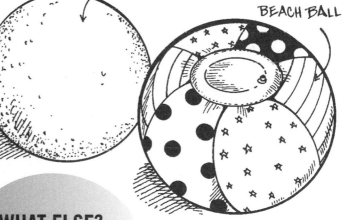

PLAYGROUND BALL

BEACH BALL

WHAT ELSE?

Play these games outside by having the children stand up as you bounce or toss the ball to them.

CHAPTER 3
Clean Up! Line Up! Let's Go!

Cleaning up, moving children to different activities, and walking to other areas in the school will become a game with the rhymes, props, and ideas in this chapter. You'll feel like the Pied Piper with the children following along!

Five-Minute Person

Use the Five-Minute Person to help children bring closure to their activities before cleanup time. This will give them a warning and prepare them for the next event.

WHAT?

no materials needed

HOW?

• Choose one child each day to be the Five-Minute Person.

• Several minutes before cleanup time, ask that child to go around the room announcing that cleanup (or any other activity) will begin in five minutes.

• The Five-Minute Person holds up five fingers and goes to each center and says, "Five more minutes."

• After five minutes, blink the lights, ring a bell, or sing a song to initiate cleanup.

WHAT ELSE?

The Five-Minute Person can also be used on the playground, during independent reading, and at other times in the school day to prepare children for the next part of the day.

Twinkle Cleanup

Sing this song to the children when it is time to clean up.

HOW?

- To guide children in picking up toys and preparing for a new activity, sing this tune and model what you want them to do.

Twinkle Clean Up (Tune: "Twinkle, Twinkle Little Star")
Twinkle, twinkle little star,
Stop and clean up where you are.
Time to put the toys away.
We'll get them out another day.
Twinkle, twinkle little star,
Stop and clean up where you are.

WHAT?

no materials needed

WHAT ELSE?

If children are not listening to you, then get their attention by singing their name in the song. For example, "Twinkle, twinkle, little Joshua, stop and clean up where you are."

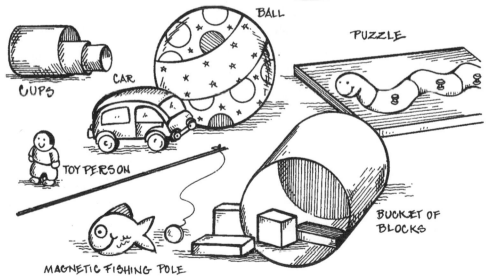

CUPS

CAR

BALL

TOY PERSON

MAGNETIC FISHING POLE

PUZZLE

BUCKET OF BLOCKS

Clean-A-Saurus

This puppet will turn clean up into a game and help the children accept responsibility.

WHAT?

felt scraps

scissors

yellow rubber glove

stapler

permanent marker

HOW?

• Use the pattern on the opposite page to cut spikes out of felt for your dinosaur puppet.

• Cut a 6" (15 cm) slit up the back of the glove, as shown. Insert the felt spikes in the slit and staple in place.

• Extend the middle finger and draw on eyes, nose, and mouth.

• After the children have tidied up, take Clean-A-Saurus around the room to check things out. If Clean-A-Saurus sees toys, books, or materials out of place, he roars to let the children know they need to correct something. The children will be eager to describe what needs to be done and fix it to make the puppet happy.

WHAT ELSE?

After you have modeled how to use Clean-A-Saurus, let the children take turns putting the puppet on their hands, and "inspecting" the room.

Use other stuffed animals and puppets to "inspect" the room.

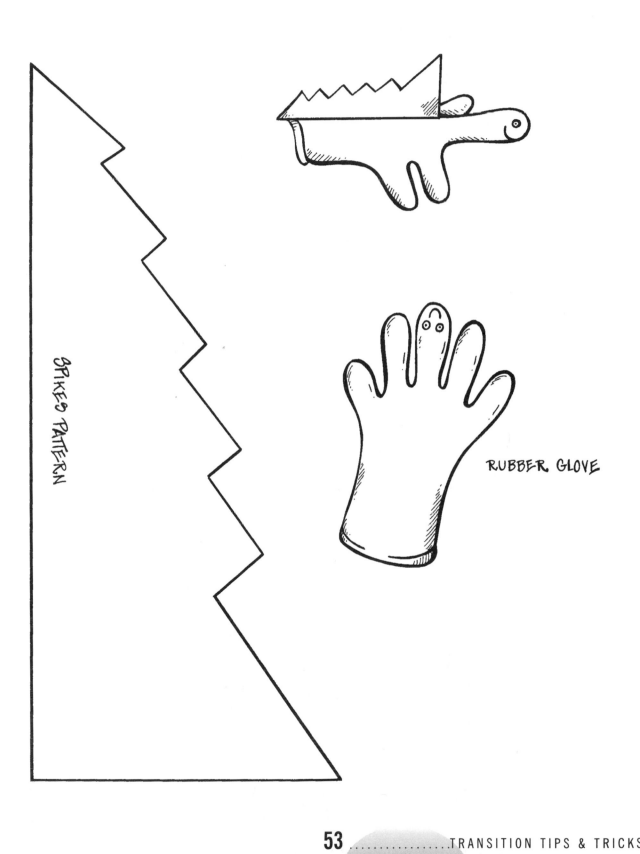

SPIKES PATTERN

RUBBER GLOVE

Say, "I Am!"

Focus children's attention and encourage them to participate with this response.

WHAT?

no materials needed

HOW?

If you want children to join in with picking up, sing the song below.

Say, "I Am!" (Tune: "If You're Happy and You Know It")
If you're cleaning up the room say, "I am."
"I am."(children respond)
If you're cleaning up the room say, "I am."
"I am." (children respond)
If you're cleaning up the room,
If you're cleaning up the room,
If you're cleaning up the room, say, "I am."
"I am." (children respond)

WHAT ELSE?

Use this chant during other transitions in the day to communicate constructively. For example:

If you're ready to go outside, say, "I am..."

If you want to hear a story, whisper, "I do..."

If you washed your hands for snack, say, "I did..."

Little Red Wagon

This little red wagon can help quietly dismiss children to a new activity. This prop will also reinforce color recognition and sequencing.

HOW?

- Using the pattern on the following page, cut the shape of a wagon out of the front of the file folder.

- Decorate around the shape of the wagon, as shown.

- Insert the paper inside the file folder, placing a red sheet on top.

- Sing the song below, removing the sheet of paper in front each time to reveal a different color.

    Little Red Wagon (Tune: "Old Brass Wagon")
    Bumping up and down in my little red wagon.
    Bumping up and down in my little red wagon.
    Bumping up and down in my little red wagon.
    Won't you be my darling?
    Bumping up and down in my little (next color) wagon...

- Tell the children that, as you reveal the color that they are wearing, they may get up and go to snack, a center, or the next activity.

WHAT?

file folder

scissors

markers

different colors of construction paper 8" x 10" (20 cm x 25 cm)

WHAT ELSE?

Always place the colored paper in the file folder in the same order, then ask children to predict which color they think will come next.

Make similar props with the shape of a car, van, bus, etc. Change the words of the song accordingly.

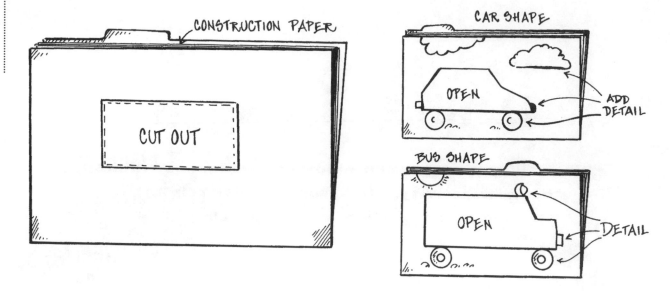

CONSTRUCTION PAPER

CUT OUT

CAR SHAPE

OPEN

ADD DETAIL

BUS SHAPE

OPEN

DETAIL

AREA TO BE CUT OUT

OPEN AREA

HANDLE

ADD BOLD BLACK OUTLINE

ADD CIRCLES FOR WHEELS

GREEN GRASS

If Your Name Begins With...

Reinforce letter recognition as you excuse the children to a new activity with this tune.

HOW?

• Tell the children to think of the letter at the beginning of their names.

• Explain that they may be dismissed when they hear that letter in the song.

If Your Name Begins With (Tune: "If You're Happy and You Know It")

If your name begins with "A" stand up.
If your name begins with "B" stand up.
If your name begins with "C" stand up.
If your name begins with "D," "E," "F," or "G,"
Then you may stand up.
If your name begins with "H" stand up...

• Continue singing other letters of the alphabet.

WHAT?

no materials needed

WHAT ELSE?

At the end of each line, sing what you want the children to do, such as "go to a center," or "sit down for snack," or "line up at the door."

Hold up letter cards as you sing the song, or point to letters on the classroom wall.

Sing letters out of sequence to improve listening skills. For example, "If your name begins with 'K' line up. If your name begins with 'D' line up...."

Ask the children to listen for the letter that their last name begins with.

Please Come and Read With Me

Sing this tune to indicate to children that it's time to begin a new activity.

WHAT?

no materials needed

HOW?

• Begin singing this song when you want to quiet children for a story:

Please Come and Read With Me (Tune: "Mary Had a Little Lamb")
Please come and read with me,
Read with me,
Read with me.
Please come and read with me,
For it's story time.

WHAT ELSE?

Change the words to fit whatever
you want children to do.
For example:

Please come and sing with me...
For it's music time.
Please come and eat with me...
For it's snack time.
Please put on your coat with me...
For it's outdoor time.

Dismissal Rhymes

Children need to listen for their names in one of these rhymes.

HOW?

- Go around the room and repeat one of these rhymes to each child:

WHAT?

no materials needed

Bibbity Bobbity Boo
Bibbity bobbity boo.
Who are you?
Bibbity bobbity B_____. (say child's name by
dropping first letter and substituting "B")
You are (child's name).
(For example: "Bibbity bobbity Bimmy.
You are Jimmy.")

Birth Date
Apples, peaches,
Oranges, plums,
Tell me when
Your birthday comes. (point to a child
who says her birthdate)

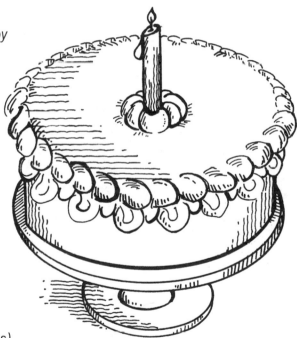

Address
Cat, dog, fish, mouse,
What is the number
On your house? (child responds with address)

Phone
Ring, ring,
Is anybody home?
What is the number
Of your telephone? (child says her phone number)

Windup Key

This prop encourages children to use their imaginations and to move in creative ways.

WHAT?

heavy cardboard

scissors

aluminum foil

HOW?

• Trace around the key pattern below on the cardboard.

• Cut it out, then cover with aluminum foil.

• Before dismissing the children to line up, show them the key.

• Explain that it is a "magic" key, and when you wind them up they can pretend to be something new.

• Here are some imaginary things they could be:

> Hopping bunnies
> Chugging trains
> Flying eagles
> Tiptoeing mice
> Dancing snowflakes
> Silly clowns
> Astronauts on the moon
> Marching soldiers
> Mad monsters
> Twirling leaves

WHAT ELSE?

Adapt movement activities to themes, stories, seasons, or holidays.

Let children take turns winding up their friends with the key.

• Slowly walk around the room as you take the key and pretend to wind up children on their backs.

• Use the key to wind up children to go to centers, snack, wash their hands, and so on.

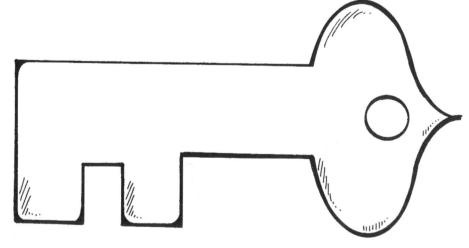

A E I O You May Be Dismissed

Dismissing children to go to a learning center or to line up becomes a game with this idea.

HOW?

- After a group activity, go around and point to each child as you say a vowel. For example, "A, E, I, O," and when you get to the fifth child say, "'U' may go to a learning center."

- Continue going around the room, pointing to children as you say, "A, E, I, O," and dismissing the child who lands on "U."

WHAT?

no materials needed

WHAT ELSE?

Change the words for whatever activity comes next. For example, "'U' may line up to go outside," or "'U' may wash your hands for snack time."

Let the children take turns tapping friends as they say the vowels.

Use one of these chants to dismiss friends:
Eeny, meeny, miney, mo.
To a center you may go.
One potato, two potato, three potato, four.
You may line up at the door.
High five. (give high five)
Down low. (slap hands down low)
Cut the pickle. (child touches finger tips, teacher pretends to "cut" in between)
Give a tickle. (teacher lightly tickles child)

Tickets, Please

Review letters, shapes, colors, or numerals with this simple game.

WHAT?

index cards

markers

HOW?

• Write the color names on the index cards, using the appropriate color marker.

• Before lining the children up or dismissing them to a new activity, shuffle the cards and pass one to each child.

• Explain that they will have to listen and when you call out the color they hold, they can hand it to you and go to the next activity.

BLUE MARKER

YELLOW MARKER

SHAPES

HINT!

Children and lines "don't mix," so avoid them whenever possible. When you do line up children, do it as quickly as possible to avoid discipline problems.

WHAT ELSE?

Use seasonal symbols to write on, such as autumn leaves, mittens, raindrops, etc.

Make a similar game using numerals or letters. Children may be dismissed when you call out the numeral they are holding.

Use animal stickers or shapes for this activity.

Play a version of Spin the Bottle to dismiss children to line up. Fill a plastic bottle with colored water, salt, or beans. Stand in the middle of the circle and spin it around. Whomever the bottle lands on may then spin the bottle and get in line. Continue until each child has had a turn to spin the bottle.

I'm Ready

This poem will help children think about appropriate behavior as they line up to move to another area in the school.

HOW?

Have children repeat this chant with you.

I'm Ready

I'm looking straight ahead of me,
I'm standing straight and tall.
I'll give myself a great, big hug,
I'm ready for the hall.
Hands on hips.
Zip up lips.
Stand up tall.
Get ready for the hall.

WHAT?

no materials needed

Get ready for the hall!

WHAT ELSE?

Write the words to this poem on a poster board and hang near the door so children can "read" it as they say it.

Marshmallow Feet

This game of pretend will engage children's imaginations and make it fun to walk quietly.

WHAT?

no materials needed

HOW?

• Before taking children out in the hall, tell them to put giant marshmallows on their feet. "Oh, and put some marshmallows in your mouths, too."

• Model this by puffing up your cheeks and walking dramatically like you have big, fluffy feet.

WHAT ELSE?

Make up other imagination games to help children move down school halls quietly. For example, you could be like "Stealth jets" and walk so quietly no other classes can detect you. Have children suggest other quiet motions.

When coming in from the playground with dirty shoes, show the children how to go, "One, two, three, cha-cha-cha." As they "cha-cha-cha," they'll be cleaning their shoes!

Put Your Feet on the Line

Adapt this tune to give children directions to line up, sit down, or change to a new activity.

HOW?

- Insert the words for what you want children to do in this song:

Put Your Feet on the Line
(Tune: "If You're Happy and You Know It")

- To line children up:

Put your feet on the line, on the line.
Put your feet on the line, on the line.
Put your feet on the line, you're looking mighty fine.
Put your feet on the line, on the line.

- To get children to sit down:

Put your seat in the chair, in the chair.
Put your seat in the chair, in the chair.
Put your seat in the chair and relax while you are there.
Put your seat in the chair, in the chair.

- To quiet children:

Put your hands in your lap, in your lap.
Put your hands in your lap, in your lap.
Put your hands in your lap, then give them a clap.
Put your hands in your lap, in your lap.

- To calm children for rest:

Put your heads on your mat, on your mat.
Put your heads on your mat, on your mat.
Close your eyes and relax,
Put your heads on your mat, on your mat.

WHAT?

no materials needed

Play Time Roundup

Here's a trick for gathering children out on the playground when it's time to return to the classroom. The children will also be learning to count.

WHAT?

no materials needed

HOW?

• When you're ready to take the children inside, simply stand by the door and raise your hand as you slowly count, "1-2-3-4-5...25."

• By the time you get to 25, the children will have joined in counting with you, and they'll all be lined up.

WHAT ELSE?

If children straggle, explain that it's a game, and the object is to get in line before you get to 25.

Count by twos, fives, tens, and so on to 100.
Count in a foreign language.

Start a class cheer to get children
in line. Clap as you say:
2-4-6-8
(Teacher's name)
Class is great!

Continue cheering until most of the children are in line. Lower your voice the final time you repeat the cheer.

CHAPTER 4

Attention Grabbers, Puppets, and Finger Fun

This chapter contains creative ways to capture children's attention with fingerplays, puppets, and rhymes that will help them focus on learning positively and quietly.

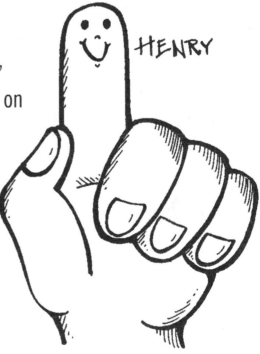

HENRY

Attention Grabbers!

Novelty is powerful, so use these ideas to capture children's minds and interests.

WHAT?

see suggestions for
each idea

HOW?

• If you want to focus children's attention for a learning activity, lesson, or story, try one of these tricks:

Change your voice—Talk in a high voice or a deep voice, or whisper.

Wear silly glasses—Get silly glasses or goggles.

Put on a hat—Wear a silly hat, cap, visor, wig, bow, etc.

Be a clown—Purchase a clown nose or other clown disguise to get a laugh.

Blow bubbles—Buy commercial bubbles or wear a bubble necklace.

Make noise—Use a clicker, whistle, or party noisemaker.

Make music—Play a music box, xylophone, bell, or other instrument.

Light up—Turn on a flashlight or flick the room lights off and on.

Cluck, bark, moo—Pretend to be an animal by mimicking the animal's sound or movements.

Wind Chime Time

Quiet children or get their attention with this pleasing sound.

HOW?

- Tell the children that you have a secret class signal that you will use when you need their attention or have something important to say to them.

- Whenever they hear that sound, they should "freeze" and look at you.

- Show them the wind chime and play it for them.

- Pass it around and let them take turns making the sound.

- Ask the children to get up and dance around.

- When you shake the wind chime, tell them to "freeze" and look at you.

- After playing this game, hang the wind chime near the door.

- Whenever you need the children's attention or need to give directions, gently shake the wind chime.

WHAT?

wind chime

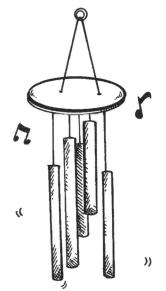

WHAT ELSE?

Use a bell, musical instrument, or other sound maker to focus children's attention.

Choose a child to be your helper and ring the wind chime.

Freddie Flea

Freddie Flea will work like magic to capture children's attention.

WHAT?

empty paper sack

WHAT ELSE?

Keep Freddie Flea in a small gift box or a little jar. Make up your own imaginary friend to entertain the children.

HOW?

- Carefully hold up the bag and explain to the children that you have a friend called Freddie Flea in the sack.

- Tell them that Freddie has tiny, little ears, so they will have to be very, very quiet before he comes out.

- Wait until all the children are still and looking at the bag, then take your right index finger, put it in the bag and say, "Come on, Freddie. The boys and girls want to see you, and they promise to be very quiet."

- Take your finger out of the bag and hold it in the air as if there is a flea on the end of it.

- Say, "Friends, this is Freddie Flea. Freddie has been practicing some tricks. Would you like to see one? Freddie can jump from one finger to the next."

- Hold up your left index finger and say, "Count softly with me and watch Freddie. One, two, three…"

- Slowly move your eyes from your right finger to the left as if there really were a flea jumping. "Would you like to see that again?" Count to three again and have Freddie return to the right finger.

- Next, tell the children that Freddie has been trying to learn how to do a flip. Again, have them count to three, then move your eyes up, in a circle, then land back on the left finger.

- After Freddie does a few more tricks, have him say good-bye to the children, then gently put him back in the sack and close the top so he "can't get out."

Henry Hush

Henry Hush will work like magic to get children's attention or calm them down.

HOW?

• Draw a little face on your index finger similar to the one illustrated.

• Wiggle Henry Hush as you sing the tune below softly:

Henry Hush (Tune: "London Bridge Is Falling Down")
Henry Hush says,
"Please be quiet,
Please be quiet,
Please be quiet."
Henry Hush says,
"Please be quiet."
Sh! Sh! Sh! (place Henry over your lips)

• If necessary, continue singing the song and lowering your voice until all the children are looking at you.

WHAT?

fine-tip marker or pen

WENDY

TINA

MUFFY

BASHFUL

WHAT ELSE?

Draw different figures on your finger and change the name. For example, you could draw Wendy Whisper, Tiny Tina, Muffy Mouse, Bashful Bunny, etc. Hide the finger with the drawing in the fist of your other hand. Tell the children you wonder who is going to come see them today. When they are quiet, slowly pull out the finger and use it to give directions.

HENRY

Paper Plate Theater

Use this miniature theater at "in-between" times in your day.

WHAT?

paper plate

scissors

fabric scraps

stapler

markers, stickers

HOW?

- Fold the plate in half and cut out half of the inner section, as shown.

- Place the plate on the fabric and trace around it so it will cover half of the plate.

- Staple the fabric to the back of the plate.

- Decorate the front with markers, stickers, and other materials.

- Use finger puppets similar to those below, stick puppets, or draw a face on your finger with a pen.

- Hold the plate in one hand and place the finger puppets on your other hand.

- Wiggle the puppets in front of the curtain. Use the puppets to give children directions, say a poem, or sing a song.

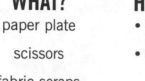

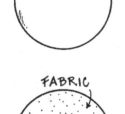

FABRIC

(CUT LARGER THAN OPENING)

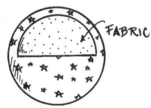

FABRIC

DECORATED FRONT

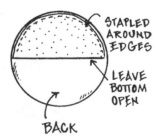

STAPLED AROUND EDGES

LEAVE BOTTOM OPEN

BACK

FINGER PUPPETS

WHAT ELSE?

Let the children make their own paper plate theaters and puppets.

Big Ears

Use this puppet to quiet children or to give them directions.

HOW?

- Make a dog from the sock by gluing on eyes, ears, a nose, and mouth, as shown.

- Cut off the top and bottom of the box.

- Pull the puppet over your hand, then put the puppet in the box.

- Tell the children you have a special friend in the box who has very sensitive ears.

- When they're quiet, stick the puppet out of the box.

- Let the children name the puppet.

- Disguise your voice to talk like the dog or have the puppet whisper in your ear and then translate for the children what the puppet has said.

- Let the puppet give the children directions or dismiss them by licking them.

- If children become too loud, simply pull the puppet back into the box.

WHAT?

old sock

felt

wiggly eyes

small black pompom

piece of red felt

glue gun

empty dog biscuit or cereal box

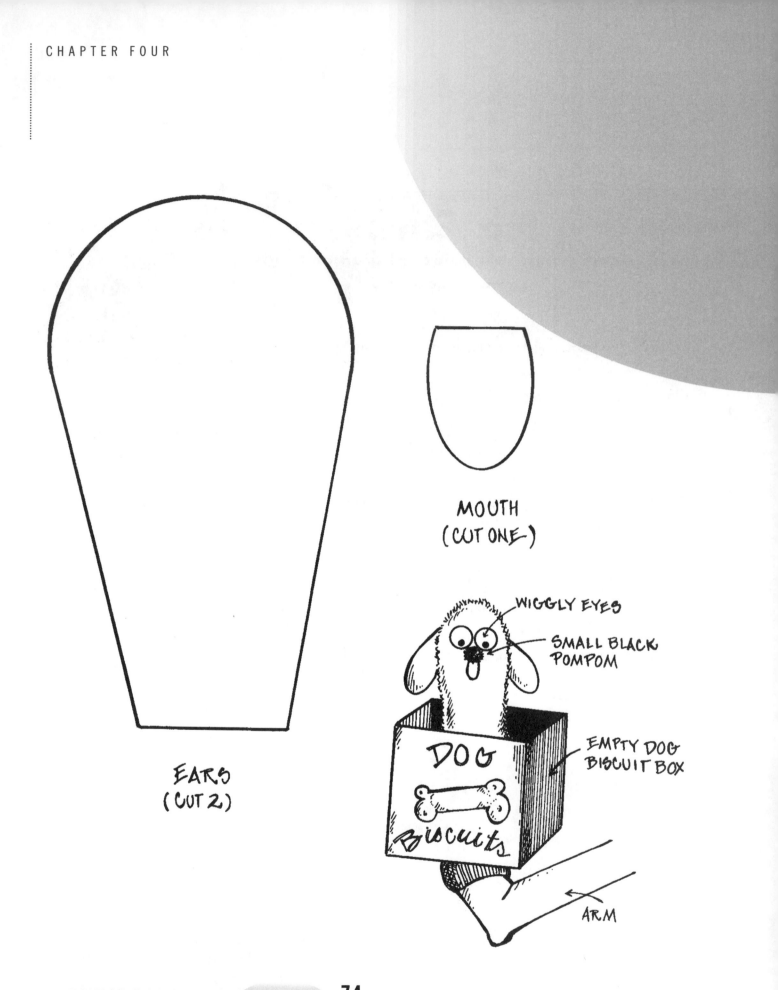

MOUTH
(CUT ONE)

EARS
(CUT 2)

WIGGLY EYES

SMALL BLACK
POMPOM

EMPTY DOG
BISCUIT BOX

DOG
Biscuits

ARM

Here Is a Turtle

Turtles are quiet, and children will be, too, with this poem.

HOW?

• Put your thumb in your fist and hold it out in front of you as you say:

Here Is a Turtle

Here is a turtle. (hold out fist)
He lives in a shell.
He likes his home
Very well.
When he gets hungry, (stick out thumb)
He comes out to eat, (wiggle thumb)
Then goes back
Into his house (tuck thumb back into fist)
To sleep.

WHAT?

no materials needed

WHAT ELSE?

How about a cup of tea?
Have a Cup of Tea (tuck thumbs in fists before you begin)
Here's a cup. (hold up right fist)
And here's a cup. (hold up left fist)
And here's a pot of tea. (stick up right thumb)
Pour a cup. (pretend to pour tea in left fist)
And pour a cup. (pour tea in right fist with left hand)
And have a cup with me. (hold up right fist, then pretend to take a drink)

Caterpillars

With this little poem, children will quiet down and get ready for what is next in the day.

WHAT?

no materials needed

LET'S GO TO SLEEP

HOW?

• To prepare children for this fingerplay, ask them to show you their little "caterpillars" as you demonstrate by wiggling your fingers in the air.

Caterpillars
"Let's go to sleep," (wiggle your fingers)
The little caterpillars said,
As they tucked themselves (interlock fingers as if praying)
Quietly in bed.
When they awake
By and by, (palms up, cross over hands)
Each one will be (clasp thumbs, and flutter fingers to make a butterfly)
A pretty butterfly.

AS THEY TUCKED THEMSELVES...

WHAT ELSE?

Have children pretend to wiggle around like caterpillars. Next ask them to spin a chrysalis and take a nap. Gently, go around and tap each child and tell him that he has become a butterfly and he can fly around the room.

. . . A PRETTY BUTTERFLY

Criss-Cross Applesauce

Remind children how to sit quietly and focus their attention on you with this rhyme.

HOW?

- Encourage the children to join in the motions as you say this poem:

Criss-Cross Applesauce
> Criss-cross applesauce,
> Give a little clap. *(clap hands)*
> Criss-cross applesauce,
> Put them in your lap. *(put hands in lap)*
>
> Criss-cross applesauce,
> Quiet as can be.
> Criss-cross applesauce,
> Eyes on me. *(point to self)*

WHAT?

no materials needed

- Use this repeatedly to let children know what behavior you expect.

- Call attention to children who are following the directions. For example, "Larry has his legs crossed and his eyes on me. I can tell he's ready to begin."

WHAT ELSE?

Use a "finger check" to distract busy fingers.

Finger Check
> 1-2-3-4-5
> *(clap hands five times as you say this)*
> 1-2-3-4-5 *(clap hands five times again)*
> Criss-cross *(cross right hand over left)*
> Applesauce. *(cross left hand over right)*
> 1-2-3-4-5 *(clap hands five times, then put them in your lap)*

Ooosha Mama Freeze!

This chant will indicate to children that it's time to stop what they're doing and focus on what you have to tell them.

WHAT?

no materials needed

HOW?

• Begin snapping your fingers as you repeat the chant below:

Miss Sue

Miss Sue, Miss Sue,
Miss Sue from Alabama,
Sitting in her rocker
Eating Betty Crocker
Watching the clock go
Tick, tock, tick, tock
Banana rock,
Ooooshamama, ooshamama,
Ooooshamama, FREEZE!

WHAT ELSE?

Give Me Five is another rhyme that grabs children's attention.

Give Me Five

Give me five. (hold up five fingers)
Two eyes. (point to eyes)
Two ears. (point to ears)
One mouth. (point to mouth)
That makes five. (whisper the last line as you hold up five fingers)

• By the time you say, "freeze," the children should have their eyes on you and be standing very still.

2-4-6-8-10

Engage all children for a new activity with this magic clap.

HOW?

• When quieting children for a story or helping them wait for everyone in the class to get ready for an activity, say:

2-4-6-8-10
> *Follow me.*
> *Two (clap two index fingers together)*
> *Four (clap index and middle fingers together)*
> *Six (clap index, middle, and ring fingers together)*
> *Eight (clap index, middle, ring, and*
> *little fingers together)*
> *Ten (clap both hands together)*

• End by silently putting your hands in your lap.

WHAT?

no materials needed

WHAT ELSE?

Do the clap forward (2-4-6-8-10) and then backward (10-8-6-4-2).

Use other clapping patterns to focus children. You might say, "Can you do this?" as you begin clapping or snapping a beat.

Let children think of clapping patterns for their friends to repeat as you wait between activities.

Listen Please!

Try one of the poems below to calm children and prepare them for the next activity.

WHAT?

no materials needed

HOW?

• Quietly repeat one of these rhymes, lowering your voice as you do so.

We Listen

We listen with our ears, of course, (point to ears)
But surely it is true,
That eyes and lips and hands and feet (point to other parts of the body)
Can surely listen, too.

Give Yourself a Hug

Give yourself a great big hug. (hug self)
Give it all you've got.
Pat yourself upon the back. (pat back)
Smile and smile a lot! (smile)

Q-U-I-E-T

Q (hold up thumb)
U (hold up index finger)
I (hold up middle finger)
E (hold up ring finger)
T (hold up little finger)
Quiet, quiet. (wave hand and whisper the last two lines)
That's what I'll be.

We Love Macaroni

Gather children for a group activity or sing this song to focus their attention.

HOW?

• Clap your hands as you begin singing:

We Love Macaroni (Tune: "Alouette")
Chorus:

Macaroni, we love macaroni. (all sing together)
Macaroni, that's what we like best.

Do you like it on your head? (teacher asks)
Yes, we like it on our head. (children respond)
On your head? (teacher asks)
On our head. (children respond)
Ohhhhhh! (teacher moans)

Chorus

Do you like it on your shirt?
Yes, we like it on our shirt.
On your shirt?
On our shirt.
On your head?
On our head.
Ohhhhhh!

Chorus

• Continue, adding the following questions:

Do you like it on your pants?
Do you like it on your socks?
Do you like it on your shoes?

WHAT?

no materials needed

WHAT ELSE?

Change "macaroni" for whatever food you are eating for lunch.

Great Ideas for Rainy Days (or any day)

As children shake and wiggle along with these rhymes and games, they develop large motor skills, release energy, and exercise their brains. Although you might remember some of these activities from your own childhood, they will be new and fresh to children today. Think of other songs and games you enjoyed as a child, and pass them on to your class. What a wonderful bridge to share between the past and the present— and between your life and theirs!

Crossover Movement

There is a line down the middle of the body, and any time
we cross over that line, we "unstick" the brain.
This activity will not only stimulate the brain,
but will also provide children with an outlet for wiggles.

WHAT?

roll of toilet paper

variety of music

HOW?

• Tear off a piece of toilet paper 18"-24" (20 cm-60 cm) long for each child.

• Ask the children to find their own space by extending their arms and turning in a circle.

• Remind children to stay in their space so they don't hit anyone else.

• Put on some music, and ask the children to do what you do.

• Hold the end of your streamer in one hand and begin making circles in front of your body. Make figure eights in front of you. Hold the streamer in your other hand and repeat.

• Make other motions with your streamer as the children follow along.

)) WHAT ELSE?

Let children take turns being the leader as they move their streamer and others copy their motions.

Experiment with different types of music. Play selections that include fast and slow music, or that are marches, lullabies, or other types of music.

Staple tissue paper or ribbon to a straw to make a colorful streamer.

Juggling

Juggling is a great way to exercise the mind and the body. It's also extra fun on a rainy day to release energy.

HOW?

- To make juggling scarves, cut the netting into 12" (30 cm) squares. (You will need two for each child.)

- Place the squares in the basket.

- To begin juggling, pass out one scarf to each child. Challenge them to throw their scarves up in the air and catch them. Let the children practice.

- Put on slow, classical music for them to juggle with.

- When children are able to juggle with one scarf, let them try it with two. Demonstrate how to "throw, throw, catch, catch," in a figure eight.

WHAT?

several yards of netting (sold at fabric stores) in different colors

scissors

basket

music

WHAT ELSE?

On sunny days, take the scarves on the playground so children can toss them to each other and practice juggling.

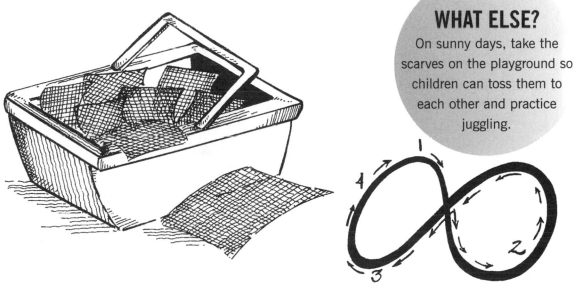

Balance Beam

Develop motor skills and coordination on a rainy day with this imaginary balance beam.

WHAT?

masking tape

HOW?

- Place the masking tape on the floor to make a 10" (25 cm) line.

- Ask children to line up and tell them to pretend the tape is like a tightrope act in the circus. Have them slowly walk across it one at a time.

- The second time, challenge them to walk backward across the tape.

- The third time, ask them to try to hop forward on one foot.

- If appropriate, continue making the task more difficult by having them walk on tiptoes, close their eyes, keep their hands by their sides, and so on.

WHAT ELSE?

Put the tape on the floor in the shape of an "S," an "8," a triangle, or other letters and geometric shapes.

Lay a jump rope on the ground out on the playground to make a balance beam game.

Use a piece of lumber on the floor as a balance beam after the children have mastered the masking tape.

Row Your Boat

Children will learn to cooperate as they develop motor skills and coordination with this game.

HOW?

- Ask the children to choose a partner and sit on the floor facing their partner with their legs extended.

- The partners touch the bottoms of their feet and hold hands.

- Show them how to slowly move back and forth with their partner as they sing the song below:

  Row, Row, Row Your Boat (Traditional Tune)
  Row, row, row your boat,
  Gently down the stream.
  Merrily, merrily, merrily, merrily,
  Life is but a dream.

- Continue singing the song slowly until children catch on to the rhythm and are moving in unison.

WHAT?

no materials needed

WHAT ELSE?

Tell them to turn up their engines and be motorboats as you sing the song a little faster.

Sing the song at different speeds and ask the children to move accordingly.

Jack Be Nimble

Jumping like "Jack" helps children get acquainted, and provides lots of fun throughout the school year.

WHAT?

small block

HOW?

- Sit in a circle.

- Place the block on the floor in the middle of the circle, and ask the children to pretend it's a candlestick.

- One at a time use children's names in the rhyme below. That child may jump over the block forward, then backward, as you say the rhyme.

Jack Be Nimble
(Child's name) be nimble.
(Child's name) be quick.
(Child's name) jump over (child jumps forward)
The candlestick.
Jump it lively,
Jump it quick.
But don't knock over (child jumps backward)
The candlestick!

WHAT ELSE?

Use a real candlestick for this game. When you have a new child join your classroom, introduce the other children with "Jack Be Nimble."

HINT!

Adapt the game to the ability of the children. Young children may only be able to jump forward. Challenge older children by stacking several blocks.

Blue Bird

This wonderful old song and game is great for a rainy day and even more fun with this little puppet.

HOW?

- Use the pattern on the following page to make a bird puppet. Cut two bodies and one pair of wings from the felt. Cut a beak out of orange or yellow felt.

- Glue the beak on one section of the body as indicated.

- Spread glue around the outside edge of this piece, leaving an opening of about 1½" (4 cm) on the bottom to insert your finger. Place the other section of the body on top.

- Cut a slit through the top of both pieces of the body, as shown. Gather wings, slip them through the slit, then open them up.

- Glue on eyes.

- Have the children stand in a circle holding hands.

- Begin the song by putting the blue bird on your finger. Weave it in and out of the children's arms, or flap your arms like a bird if you do not have a bird puppet.

WHAT?

blue felt

scissors

scrap of orange or yellow felt

two wiggly eyes

glue gun or fabric glue

WHAT ELSE?

This puppet can also be used to "peck" children to dismiss them to a new activity.

Use the blue bird to help children track a line of print.

Blue Bird Through My Window (Traditional Tune)

Blue bird, blue bird,
Through my window.
Blue bird, blue bird,
Through my window.
Blue bird, blue bird,
Through my window,
Oh, (child's name), (say child's name you are near)
I'm so tired.
Find a little friend (tap the puppet on that child's shoulder)
And tap them on the shoulder.
Find a little friend
And tap them on the shoulder.
Find a little friend (pass puppet to that child who exchanges
  places with you)
And tap them on the shoulder.
Oh, (child's name),
I'm so tired.

- Continue the song with the child using the bird puppet.

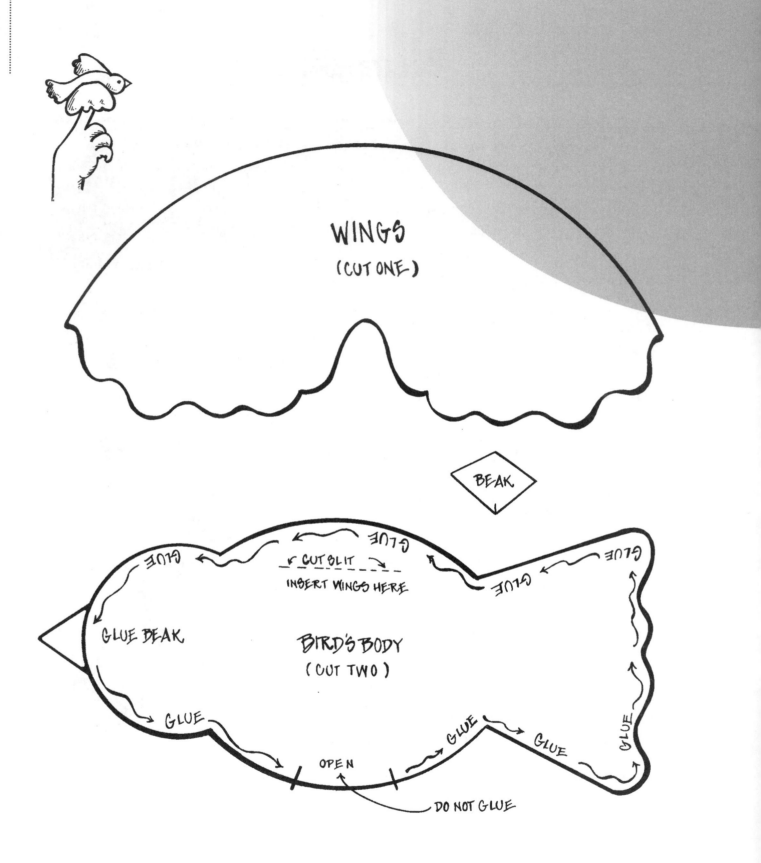

WINGS
(CUT ONE)

BEAK

GLUE
GLUE
→ CUT SLIT →
INSERT WINGS HERE
GLUE
GLUE
GLUE BEAK
BIRD'S BODY
(CUT TWO)
GLUE
GLUE
GLUE
GLUE
OPEN
DO NOT GLUE

London Bridge

This game requires no special skills and is a favorite of children of all ages. Although it has been around for years, the game is new, fresh, and exciting for children who have never experienced it.

HOW?

- Choose two children to be the bridge. They face each other.

- Show them how to hold hands and extend their arms in the air.

- The other children line up and walk in single file under the bridge as you sing:

> **London Bridge (Traditional Tune)**
> *London Bridge is falling down,*
> *Falling down, falling down.*
> *London Bridge is falling down,*
> *My fair lady. (the two bridge children bring their arms down and "capture" another child)*
> *Take the keys and lock her up, (the bridge children gently swing this third child back and forth)*
> *Lock her up, lock her up.*
> *Take the keys and lock her up,*
> *My fair lady.*

- The child who was "caught" takes the place of one child who was part of the bridge and the game continues.

WHAT?

no materials needed

WHAT ELSE?

Children who are caught stand behind one of the two children who are the bridge until all the children are "caught."

Lassie and Laddie

Children will enjoy being the leader while their friends try to mimic their motions in this song.

WHAT?

no materials needed

HOW?

- Explain to the children that in Scotland boys are called "laddies" and girls are called "lassies."

- Ask the children to stand in a circle, then choose a girl to get in the middle.

- Ask everyone if the child in the middle is a lassie or laddie, then sing the song below as the child in the middle jumps, hops, dances, or another motion of her choice. The other children mimic the motions of the child in the middle.

Did You Ever See a Lassie? (Traditional Tune)

Did you ever see a lassie,
A lassie, a lassie?
Did you ever see a lassie
Go this way and that?
Go this way, and that way,
And this way, and that way.
Did you ever see a lassie
Go this way and that?

- The lassie (girl) in the middle then chooses a laddie (boy) to take her place, as you sing:

  Did you ever see a
  laddie, a laddie, a laddie...

- The game continues until all children have had a turn being lassie or laddie.

Let's Do a Little Twirling

Children naturally stimulate their brains as they wiggle and play. Twirling, jumping, rocking, marching, and other gross motor movements are other enjoyable ways to exercise the brain (and the body).

HOW?

• Remind the children how important it is to exercise and how much their brains love to move. Demonstrate each of the verses, having the children follow along.

Let's Do a Little Twirling (Tune: "We Wish You a Merry Christmas")
Let's all do a little twirling, (children stand and slowly spin around)
Let's all do a little twirling,
Let's all do a little twirling,
To exercise our brains.

• Insert the following words in the song. Do the motions as you sing the song.

Hopping
Jumping
Marching
Rocking
Running
Swimming

WHAT?

no materials needed

WHAT ELSE?

Let children suggest other movements and demonstrate them as their friends follow along.

Write the motions on paper plates or strips of poster board. Hold them up as you sing them.

There Was a Wise Teacher

Use this version of an old song to exercise children on a rainy day (or any day).

WHAT?

no materials needed

HOW?

• Have the children stand up and do what you do:

There Was a Wise Teacher (Tune: "The Noble Duke of York")
*There was a wise teacher. (begin marching in place and
    swinging your arms)
She had so many children.
She marched them up the hall,
And she marched them down again. (stoop down)
And when you're up, you're up. (stand up tall)
And when you're down, you're down. (stoop down)
And when you're only halfway up, (bend knees slightly)
You're neither up, nor down. (stand up, then down)*

• Sing the song slowly and move accordingly.

• Sing fast and move quickly.

• Mouth the words as you do the motions.

Sunshine Band

Chase away the clouds and rain with your very own sunshine band. The noise may wake up the whole school, but marching is a good way to stimulate the brain.

HOW?

- Make a paper hat for each child from newspaper or newsprint, following the directions below.

- To decorate the hats use crayons, markers, or art scraps and glue.

- Next, have each child choose a musical instrument. (If you don't have enough to go around, give them blocks to tap, or two paper plates to use like cymbals.)

- Let the children put on their hats and march around the room as you play some lively music or sing the song below.

Sunshine Band (Tune: "Old MacDonald")
(Teacher's name) had a band.
E I E I O.
And we are that Sunshine Band.
E I E I O.
So all join in,
Put on a grin.
We're on our way.
It's a happy day.
We are the Sunshine Band.
E I E I O.

WHAT?

newspaper or newsprint

markers, crayons, or paper scraps and glue

musical instruments

lively music

WHAT ELSE?

March around the halls of your school and add a little novelty and joy to the other classes!

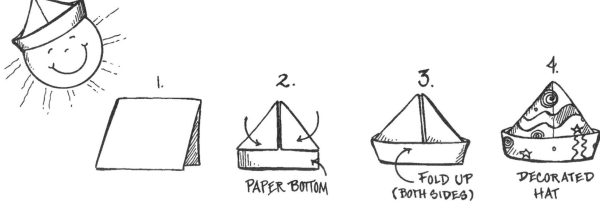

1.

2. PAPER BOTTOM

3. FOLD UP (BOTH SIDES)

4. DECORATED HAT

Ride That Pony

Encourage friendships and coordination with this movement game.

WHAT?

no materials needed

HOW?

- Each child faces a partner as she says the chant below and mirrors her partner's movements.

Ride That Pony

Ride, ride, ride that pony. (clap hands with partner and bounce up and down to the beat)
Get up and ride that big pony.
Ride, ride, ride that pony.
This is what they told me. (slap thighs to beat)
Up, up, up, my pony…(slap hands with partner, up high, to the beat)
Down, down, down, my pony…(slap hands with partner, down low, to the beat)
Around, and around, my pony…(turn around to the beat)

WHAT ELSE?

Have children stand in concentric circles. At the end of each verse, the inside circle steps to the right and the outside circle steps to the left, and everyone will have a new partner.

- Everyone scurries to find a new partner as you begin saying the chant again. Continue until children lose interest.

Chugga Chugga

Here's another movement chant children will beg to do over and over. It can also be used when children are waiting for the next activity.

HOW?

- Have children stand in a line behind you as you begin saying the chant and modeling the movements.

Chugga Chugga Chant

Ms. (Teacher's name) (clap hands and move side to side)
Has a real cool class.
They've got a lot of this,
    (stick out pointer finger on each hand and dance)
And a lot of that.
So come on now and get up,
    (shake pointer fingers up in the air to the beat)
Chugga-chugga-chugga,
Chugga-chug-chug.
Get down chugga-chugga,
    (shake pointer fingers down to the floor)
Chugga-chug-chug.
To the left chugga-chugga,
    (shake fingers as you slide to the left)
Chugga-chug-chug.
To the right chugga-chugga,
    (shake fingers as you slide to the right)
Chugga-chug-chug.

WHAT?

no materials needed

Robots

As children pretend to be robots they develop large motor skills and coordination.

WHAT?

no materials needed

HOW?

• Have children stand and follow along as you say the chant below in a mechanical, staccato voice.

Robots

What would you do if you went to robot school?
Just look at me, and a robot you will be.
   Robots at attention. (stand at attention)
   Robots, let's begin.
    Right arm. (start moving right arm up and down)
What would you do if you went to robot school?
Just look at me, and a robot you will be.
Robots at attention. (stand at attention)
 Robots, let's begin.
      Right arm. (start moving right arm up and down)
      Left arm... (move left arm up and down, too)

• Continue, adding the following motions:

Right foot. (move right foot up and down)
Left foot. (move left foot up and down)
Head up. Head down. (move head up and down)
Tongue in. Tongue out. (stick tongue in and out)
Turn around. (turn around as you do the other motions)
Robots sit down. (end chant by having children sit down)

Mother Goony Bird

Wiggle and chant any time during the day with Mother Goony Bird.

HOW?

• Have children stand and follow along as you chant and make the motions below:

Mother Goony Bird

> *Mother Goony Bird had seven chicks,*
> *And seven chicks had Mother Goony Bird,*
> *And they couldn't swim, "No." (shake head)*
> *And they couldn't fly. "No." (shake head)*
> *All they did was go like this,*
> *Right arm. (flap right arm like a wing)*
> *Mother Goony Bird...(flap right arm, then left arm)*
> *Right arm, left arm.*
> *Continue adding right foot... (stomp right foot, then left foot, then nod your head)*
> *Left foot...*
> *Nod your head...*

• On the last verse say:

> *Turn around sit down. (turn around and sit down)*

• Try singing this to "Father Abraham."

WHAT?

no materials needed

WHAT ELSE?

Lower your voice as you sing the last verse so children will automatically sit down and be quiet.

Popcorn

Children will have to listen and respond as they jump up in this poem.

WHAT?

no materials needed

HOW?

• Ask the children if they've ever seen popcorn popping in a pan. What happens? Explain that they get to be like little popcorn kernels.

• Every time they hear the word "Pop!" they get to jump up and clap their hands over their heads.

• Begin by asking the children to squat down on the floor and repeat this rhyme with you.

Popcorn

Five little kernels sizzling in the pot.
The grease got hot and one went "Pop!" (children jump up)
Four little kernels sizzling in the pot.
The grease got hot and one went "Pop!" (children jump up)
Three...
Two...
One...
No little kernels sizzling in the pot.
The pot got hot and it went "Pop!" (children jump up)

WHAT ELSE?

Have the children hold up five fingers and say this fingerplay with you. They can clap their hands on the word "Pop!"

Write the words to this rhyme on a language experience chart. Have the children track the words as you read it together.

Space Ball

Children release energy and practice eye-hand coordination with this recycled ball.

HOW?

- Cut off one leg of the pantyhose from the knee down.

- Take the remaining leg and panty section and stuff it down into the toe of the leg you cut off.

- Tie a knot around the ball you have made in the toe.

- Toss the ball across the room and watch it sail like something in space.

- Let the children toss it up and try to catch it individually, or toss it to a friend.

- Place a box or basket in the center of the room, and encourage the children to try to toss their space balls in the box.

WHAT?

old pantyhose (washed, of course!)

scissors

box or basket

WHAT ELSE?

Have children bring in old pantyhose from home and make their own space balls.

Let them decorate them with markers and fringe the tails.

Ask children to create their own games to play with their space balls.

OLD PANTY HOSE

CUT

Can Catch

This simple toy made from recycled materials is sure to please the children.

WHAT?

empty potato chip canister

tennis ball

HOW?

• Demonstrate how to bounce the tennis ball, then catch it in the can.

• Challenge the children to count how many times they can do it in a row.

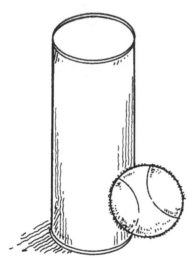

WHAT ELSE?

Give several children cans. Let them take turns bouncing the ball as their friends try to catch it. The one to catch the ball gets to bounce it the next time.

Have children paint their cans or cover them with wallpaper scraps.

HINT:

Tennis centers may donate old tennis balls to your classroom.

BALL BOUNCING INTO CAN

DECORATED CAN

Paddle Ball

It's a rainy day and you're out of ideas! Try this simple game to release energy and develop eye-hand coordination.

HOW?

- Let each child decorate two paper plates with crayons.

- Cut a small curve out of one plate as shown, then staple the two plates together.

- Wad up a piece of scrap paper and wrap masking tape around it to make a ball.

- Children insert their hand in the paper plate and use it like a bat to hit the ball.

- After children have practiced, they may try to volley the ball back and forth with a friend.

WHAT?

paper plates

crayons

scissors

stapler

scrap paper

masking tape

WHAT ELSE?

Paddle ball can also be played on the playground.

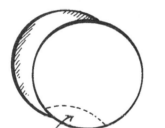

CUT OFF (ONE PLATE ONLY)

STAPLES

HAND INSIDE

ARM

MASKING TAPE BALL

CHAPTER 6

Sing, Rhyme, and Chant!

According to brain research, the brain loves rhythm, rhyme, and music. In addition, early literacy research emphasizes the significant role songs and chants play in helping children develop language and reading skills. But children love music just because it's fun and makes them feel good. So whenever you sing one of the songs or say one of these chants, remind yourself that you are not only having fun with the children, you are also stimulating children's brains and nurturing language skills! Double the fun by making the props to go along with these activities.

Jukebox

Keep this jukebox handy for when you need a song or chant.

WHAT?

small box

glue

construction paper

markers

index cards

HOW?

• Cover the box with construction paper.

• Decorate with musical notes and write "Jukebox" on it.

• Cut out words to the titles of songs, such as "Twinkle, Twinkle Little Star" or "If You're Happy and You Know It" and glue the words in the title of one song to each index card. (Or you can write the title of one song on each index card.)

• Place the cards in the box.

• Whenever you have a few extra minutes, spin a tune on the jukebox.

• Hand a child a pretend quarter. Instruct him to put it in the box and pull out a song.

• The class then sings that song.

HINT!
Make copies of the songs in this chapter and use them in the jukebox.

HOLE FOR QUARTER

WHAT ELSE?

You can continue giving children "quarters" and singing the songs they select as long as they are interested.

Cut paper in the shape of CDs and write the titles of the songs on them.

Make a similar activity using nursery rhymes.

Rhythm Sticks

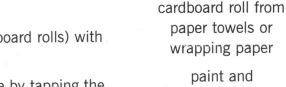

Entertain children and reinforce patterning skills with homemade rhythm sticks.

HOW?

• Each child will need two cardboard rolls.

• Let children decorate their own rhythm sticks (cardboard rolls) with paint, markers, or other art media.

• Play some music and demonstrate how to keep time by tapping the rhythm sticks together.

• Ask children to suggest other ways they could make music with their sticks. For example, you could tap the floor, tap them above your head, tap them on your shoulders, and so forth. Let the children experiment with the sticks.

• Ask the children if they know what a pattern is. Explain that a pattern is something you do over and over, and that you can tap out a pattern with rhythm sticks. For example, you can tap the floor, then tap together, tap the floor, then tap together. Demonstrate, then have the children join in with you.

• Let the children make up different patterns to do with the sticks.

WHAT?

cardboard roll from paper towels or wrapping paper

paint and paintbrushes, markers, crayons, or stickers

music

WHAT ELSE?

Play a variety of music for the children to use with their rhythm sticks. You might use a classical piece, music from around the world, jazz, show tunes, folk music, and other styles. Ask children to describe the music and how it makes them feel.

Fill film containers with rice, beans, paper clips, pebbles, and other objects to make musical shakers.

CARDBOARD ROLLS

Here We Go Round the Days of the Week

Gross motor movements, such as jumping, twirling, marching, running, and hopping, all stimulate the brain. So use this song to "boost" the brain and reinforce days of the week.

WHAT?

paper plates

markers

7 paint sticks

tape

HOW?

- Print the days of the week and motions on the paper plates, as shown.

- Write numerals on the backs to indicate numerical order.

- Tape plates to the paint sticks.

- Pass out the plates to seven children, then help them get in order from left to right.

- Tell them when they hear the children in the class sing the name of the day that is written on their paper plate, they should hold up their plate.

- Read over the days of the week and the action words on the plates before singing the song below.

  Here We Go Round (Tune: "Here We Go Round the Mulberry Bush")

  This is the way we twirl around, (slowly spin around)
  Twirl around, twirl around.
  This is the way we twirl around,
  So early Sunday morning.
  This is the way we jump up and down... (jump)
  This is the way we swim around... (swim)
  This is the way we run around... (run in place)
  This is the way we hop up and down... (hop on one foot)
  This is the way we dance around... (silly dance)
  This is the way we sit right down... (sit down)

I'm a Nut

Put a smile on your face with this silly tune.

HOW?

• Have the children join in as you sing:

I'm a Nut (Tune: "I'm a Little Piece of Tin")
I'm a little acorn brown
Lying on the cold, cold, ground.
Everybody steps on me,
That is why I'm cracked you see.

Chorus:
I'm a nut. Click! Click! (click tongue)
I'm a nut. Click! Click! (move head from side to side as you
  make a clicking noise)
I'm a nut, I'm a nut,
I'm a nut. Click! Click!

Called myself up on the phone (pretend to hold phone)
Just to see if I was home.
Asked myself out on a date.
Said to be ready about half past eight.

Chorus

WHAT?

no materials needed

WHAT ELSE?

Bring in a real acorn for the children to investigate. How does it look like a person?

Twinkling Stars

Rest time, rainy days, or gloomy times will brighten with these glow-in-the-dark stars.

WHAT?

craft sticks

glow-in-the-dark stars

glue or glue gun

HINT!
This is a good opportunity to help children who are fearful of the dark by talking about all the fun things you can do when it's dark.

HOW?

• Glue a star to each craft stick.

• Pass one to each child and demonstrate how to wave it around as you sing:

Twinkle, Twinkle, Little Star (Traditional Tune)
Twinkle, twinkle, little star.
How I wonder what you are?
Up above the world so high.
Like a diamond in the sky.
Twinkle, twinkle, little star.
How I wonder what you are?

• Tell the children that you are going to turn off the lights and close the blinds to darken the room. Explain that something magic will happen to their stars.

• Sing the song again in the dark as the children wave and "twinkle" their stars.

WHAT ELSE?
Insert extra stars in a plastic bottle. Fill with water and glue on the lid with a glue gun. Let a child who is having trouble relaxing at rest play with the bottle.

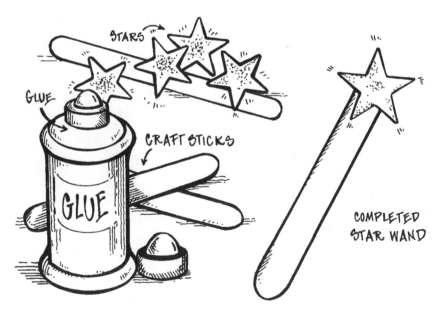

STARS

GLUE

CRAFT STICKS

GLUE

COMPLETED STAR WAND

Color Word Song

Here's a song to reinforce colors, word recognition, and letters.

HOW?

- Cut the poster board into 5" x 10" (12.5 cm x 25 cm) rectangles.

- Write the following words with the matching color of marker on the rectangles.

red	blue	green
orange	purple	yellow

- Hold up the cards and point to the letters as you sing the different verses in this song.

Color Word Song (Tune: "BINGO")

There was a farmer had a hen and RED was her name-o
R - E - D, R - E - D, R - E - D,
And RED was her name-o.

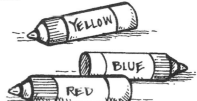

- Continue with other verses, spelling out the colors as you point to the letters.

There was a farmer had a bird and BLUE was his name-o...
There was a farmer had a turtle and GREEN was her name-o...
There was a farmer had a fish and ORANGE was his name-o...
There was a farmer had a cow and PURPLE was her name-o...
There was a farmer had a duck and YELLOW was his name-o...

WHAT?

poster board

scissors

markers

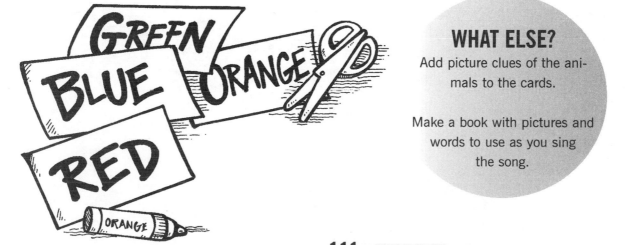

WHAT ELSE?

Add picture clues of the animals to the cards.

Make a book with pictures and words to use as you sing the song.

Barnyard Friends

This animal necklace will capture children's fancy and can be used in many different songs.

WHAT?

felt scraps

scissors

small wiggly eyes

fabric glue or glue gun

8 spring clothespins

30" (75 cm) piece of ribbon

HOW?

• Use the patterns on page 133 to cut animals out of felt.

• Decorate with wiggly eyes and felt scraps.

• Glue one animal to each clothespin.

• Make a necklace by tying the ends of the ribbon together and wearing it around your neck.

• Attach the clothespins to the necklace as you sing about the different animals in the song below.

Barnyard Friends (Tune: "Down by the Station")
See the little (pigs) (vary animals and sounds)
Down in the barnyard.
If you do not feed them,
This is what they'll say,
"Oink-oink, oink-oink, oink-oink."
See the little (cows)-(cats)-(horses)-(ducks), etc.

WHAT ELSE?

Use these same animals for "Old MacDonald Had a Farm," the "Farmer in the Dell," "I Had a Cat," etc. This visual can also be used to tell the story of "The Little Red Hen."

Make a simple version of this necklace from paper by coloring the animals on page 133, laminating them, and gluing them to the clothespins.

Play a visual memory game with the animals. Attach four or five to your necklace. Tell the children to close their eyes and remove one animal. When they open their eyes, have them make the sound of the animal that is missing.

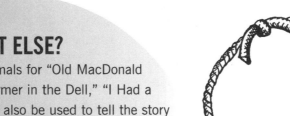

CLOTHESPIN

Five Little Fish

Everyone will want to pretend to be in this "school" of fish.

HOW?

- Decorate each sock to look like a fish by cutting out the felt pieces for fins, mouths, and eyes on the following page.

- Glue these to the socks as shown. (The more colorful and silly looking, the better!)

- Choose five children to wear the socks on their hands and be the fish.

- Tell them when you point to them they may get up and "swim" around the room.

- The other children can use their fingers to sing the song.

WHAT?

5 old socks

felt scraps

glue gun or fabric glue

Five Little Fish (Tune: "Down in the Meadow by the Itty Bitty Pool")
One little fishie swimming in the sea, (hold up one finger)
Splishing and a splashing (pretend to swim)
And a rocking to the beat.
Here comes another fish
Oh, say "Hello," (wave)
Two little fishies (hold up two fingers)
And away they go.
Two little fishies swimming in the sea...
Three little fishies...
Four little fishies...
Five little fishies swimming in the sea (hold up five fingers)
Splishing and a splashing
And a rocking to the beat.
Here comes a shark, (put palms of hands together and pretend
* to swim like a shark)*
And don't you know,
Five little fishies have to go! (wave good-bye)

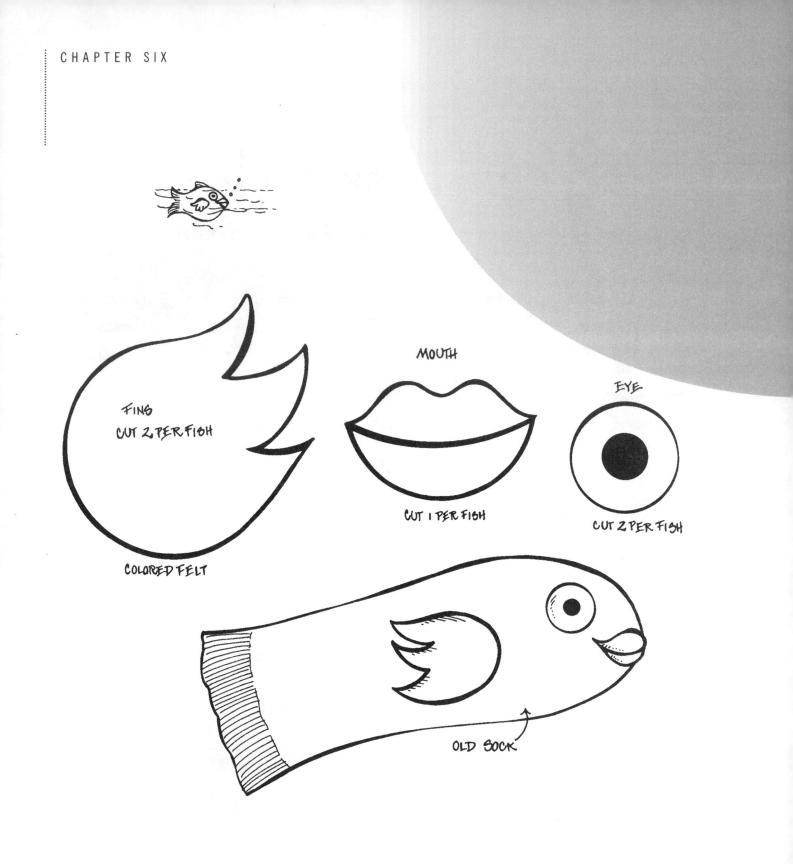

FINS
CUT 2 PER FISH

COLORED FELT

MOUTH

CUT 1 PER FISH

EYE

CUT 2 PER FISH

OLD SOCK

Five Little Birds

This is an adaptation of an old favorite of children. Make the puppet to add to the fun.

HOW?

- Cut the five fingers off the glove.

- Trace around the wings, beak, and eye patterns below and glue them on the fingers of the glove to make bird puppets.

- Place the little birds on your fingers as you begin to sing:

Five Little Birds (Tune: "Five Little Ducks Went Out to Play")
Five little birdies sitting in the tree. (hold up five fingers)
One flew away with a "Tweet, tweet, tweet." (remove one bird)
Mother bird said, "It's time to rest.
Come right back to our nest."
Four little birdies (then three, two, one…)
No little birdies sitting in the tree. (hold up fist)
They all flew away with a "tweet, tweet, tweet."
Mother bird said, "It's time to eat."
And they all flew back with a "Tweet, tweet, tweet!"
(hold up five fingers and put puppets back on fingers)

WHAT?

cloth glove

scissors

felt scraps

felt-tip pens

fabric glue

WHAT ELSE?

Choose five children to be baby birds and one child to be the mother. Let them act out the song as you sing.

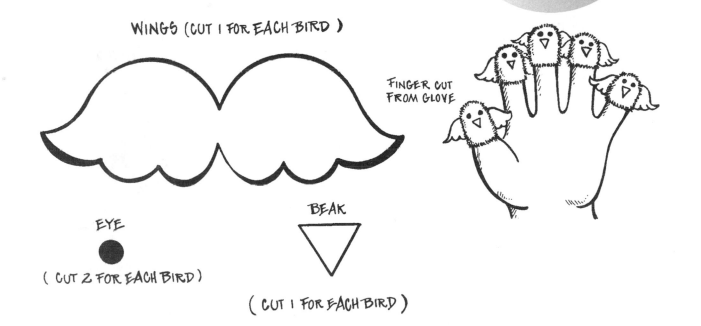

WINGS (CUT 1 FOR EACH BIRD)

FINGER CUT FROM GLOVE

EYE

(CUT 2 FOR EACH BIRD)

BEAK

(CUT 1 FOR EACH BIRD)

Speckled Frogs

Children will enjoy singing or saying this chant and acting it out.

WHAT?

green construction
paper

scissors

crayons

wooden craft sticks

tape

cardboard roller from
paper towels

WHAT ELSE?

Choose five children to
be the frogs and act
out the rhyme.

HOW?

• Cut out five frogs from construction paper using the pattern on the
opposite page. Color.

• Break the craft sticks in half. Tape a frog to each half.

• Color the cardboard roller brown to look like a log.

• Cut five slits along one side of the roll. Insert a popsicle stick in each
slit so it looks like the frogs are sitting on the log.

• Sing the song below, removing frogs as indicated in the song.

Five Speckled Frogs (Traditional Tune)
Five little speckled frogs, (children hold up five fingers)
Sitting on a speckled log,
Eating some most delicious bugs (pat tummy)
Yum! Yum!
One jumped into the pool, (remove a frog)
Where it was nice and cool, (wrap arms around self)
Now there are four little speckled frogs. (hold up four fingers)
Four little speckled frogs... (then three, two, one...)
No little speckled frogs. (make a zero with fingers)
Glump! Glump!

WOODEN CRAFT STICK   SLIT

CARDBOARD ROLLER FROM PAPER TOWELS

The Gumball

Children will be so engaged with this tongue twister, they won't realize they are developing phonological skills.

WHAT?

no materials needed

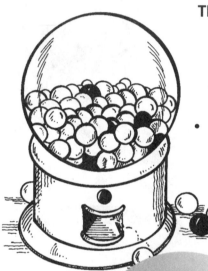

HOW?

• Teach the children the chant below:

The Gumball

I put the penny in the gum slot.
I watched the gum roll down.
I get the gum and you get the wrapper,
Cause I put the penny in the gum slot.

• Chant it again changing the beginning letter of each word. For example, using "b" the song would go:

Bi but be benny bin be bum bot.
Bi batched be bum boll bown.
Bi bet be bum band bou bet be bapper,
Bause bi but be benny bin be bum bot.

• Continue inserting different consonants in the tune.

WHAT ELSE?

Write the song on a language experience chart or overhead projector. Make additional copies of other verses.

Singing the ABCs

Here are some creative, new versions of the traditional alphabet song. Sing to gather children for circle time, while waiting in line, as you wash your hands, or at other "in-between" times.

HOW?

• Slowly sing the "Alphabet Song" using one of these ideas:

The Alphabet Song (Traditional Tune)
A B C D E F G H I J K L M N O P
Q R S T U V W X Y Z
Now I've said my ABCs,
Next time won't you sing with me?

Monster version—Sing with a loud voice.
Mouse version—Sing with a high, squeaky voice.
Opera version—Sing dramatically with outstretched arms.
Backward version—Turn around and sing.
Upside down version—Put head on the floor and sing.
With a cold version—Hold nose and sing.
Underwater version—Put finger between lips and wiggle.
Z Y X version—Sing backward from Z to A (very hard!).
Silent version—Mouth the words with no sound.

WHAT?

no materials needed

HINT!
Be sure to enunciate each letter distinctly so they don't blend together.

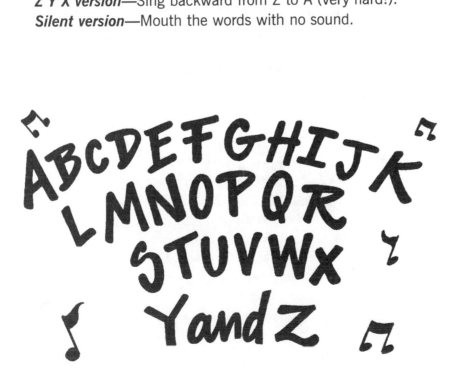

I Know an Old Lady

Auditory memory and sequence skills will be nurtured with this traditional favorite.

WHAT?

poster board

scissors

plastic baggie

tape

string

construction paper

markers

HOW?

• Cut the poster board into the shape of a dress similar to the one on the next page.

• Cut a 6" (15 cm) hole out of the center and tape the baggie to the back of the hole.

• Tie a 20" (50 cm) piece of string to the top so you can hang it around your neck as you sing the song.

• Color and cut out the animals on page 122 and insert them into the old lady's tummy as you sing.

I Know an Old Lady (Traditional Tune)

I know an old lady who swallowed a fly. (insert fly)
I don't know why she swallowed the fly,
Perhaps she'll cry.
I know an old lady who swallowed a spider. (insert spider)
That wiggled and jiggled and tickled inside her.
She swallowed the spider to catch the fly...
I know an old lady who swallowed a bird. (insert bird)
How absurd to swallow a bird...
I know an old lady who swallowed a cat. (insert cat)
Imagine that, she swallowed a cat!...
I know an old lady who swallowed a dog. (insert dog)
What a hog to swallow a dog...
I know an old lady who swallowed a goat. (insert goat)
Just opened her throat and swallowed that goat...
I know an old lady who swallowed a cow. (insert cow)
I don't know how she swallowed a cow!...
I know an old lady who swallowed a horse. (insert horse)
This is a silly song, of course!

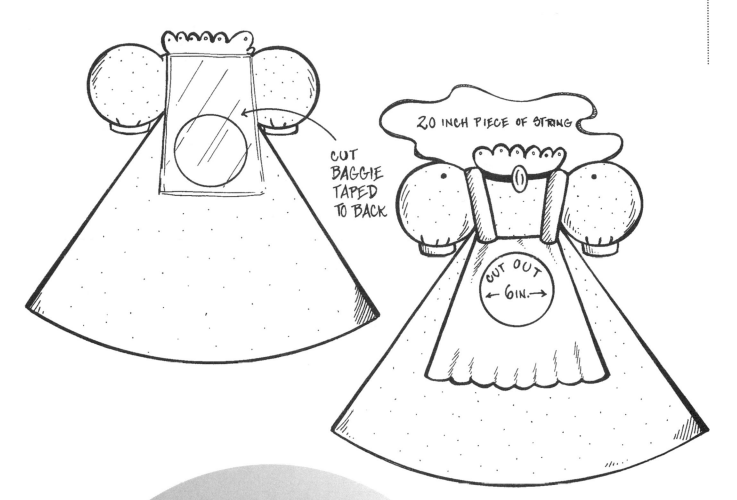

CUT BAGGIE TAPED TO BACK

20 INCH PIECE OF STRING

CUT OUT 6 IN.

WHAT ELSE?

Let children take turns wearing the "old lady" and inserting the items as they are sung.

Have children make their own visual for this song. Let them decorate a paper lunch sack to look like the "old lady." Give them copies of the animals to color and cut out. As they sing the song they can drop the pictures in the sack.

Make the characters for this song out of felt and place them on a felt board as you sing.

Have children make up their own verses for this song with other silly things the lady could eat. For example: "I know an old lady who swallowed a snake, and all she did was shiver and shake"; or "I know an old lady who swallowed a dinosaur; then her mouth let out a roar."

Clocks

Children love the exaggeration of this rhyme, and it's great to reinforce concepts about size.

HOW?

- Begin this fingerplay by demonstrating how to be a big clock by making a circle above your head with your arms.

Clocks

> Big clocks go *(hands over head in a circle)*
> Tick, tock *(say with a loud, deep, slow voice)*
> Tick, tock.
> Tick, tock.
> Medium size clocks go *(touch thumbs and fingers on opposite hands)*
> Tick, tock *(say in an average voice at a medium speed)*
> Tick, tock.
> Tick, tock.
> And little tiny clocks go *(make a small circle with index finger and thumb)*
> Tick, tock *(say slowly in a high, squeaky voice)*
> Tick, tock
> Tick, tock

WHAT?

no materials needed

WHAT ELSE?

Say other rhymes with a deep voice, high voice, fast, slow, loud, soft, and so on.

Bubble Gum

Laugh and wiggle as you repeat this chant.

WHAT?

no materials needed

HOW?

• Tell the children to pretend to get out their bubble gum, unwrap it, put it in their mouths and begin to chew.

Bubble Gum

> Bubble gum, bubble gum, (roll hands around)
> Sticky, sticky, sticky, bubble gum,
> And it sticks right to my head. (put hands on head and pretend to pull away)
> So I pull,
> And I pull,
> And I PULL! (pull free of head)

• Pretend to stick bubble gum to other body parts, such as your stomach, feet, face, etc.

• End by having the children pretend to put their bubble gum back in the wrapper and throw it away in the trash can.

A Chubby Snowman

This poem will warm children's hearts on a cold winter day.

HOW?

- Color and cut out the snowman pattern, or make your own version.

- Cut out the finger hole in the middle of the snowman's face, and also cut a 2" (5 cm) circle out of the side of the cup.

- Tape the snowman to the cup, matching up circles. Insert the cup over your hand, sticking your index finger through the hole to make the snowman's nose.

WHAT?

copy of the snowman
(see illustration)

markers

scissors

tape

plastic or paper cup
(not Styrofoam)

A Chubby Snowman

> A chubby little snowman (wiggle puppet's nose)
> Had a carrot for a nose.
> Along came a bunny,
> And what do you suppose? (hand on hip)
> That hungry little bunny
> Looking for some lunch,
> Ate that little snowman's nose, (slowly pull your
>   index finger inside the cup)
> Nibble, nibble, crunch!

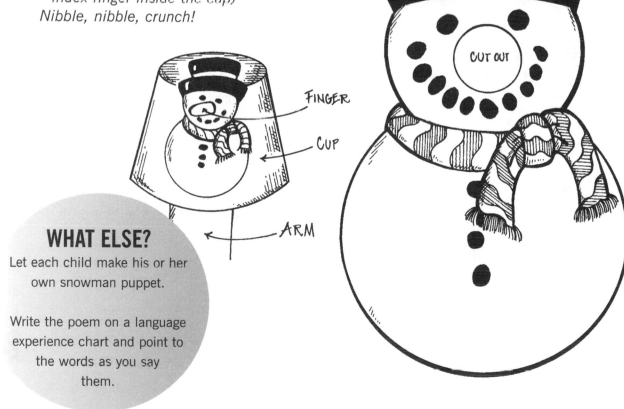

WHAT ELSE?

Let each child make his or her own snowman puppet.

Write the poem on a language experience chart and point to the words as you say them.

Here's a Bunny

**Here's a funny bunny that's easy to make
and sure to please little ones.**

WHAT?

small paper cup

paper

crayons

scissors

straw

tape

HOW?

- Color and cut out the rabbit pattern on the bottom of the page and tape to the end of the straw.

- Poke a hole in the bottom of the cup and insert the straw so the rabbit is in the cup, as shown.

- As you begin the poem, push the straw up so the children can see the rabbit.

- At the end, pull the straw down so it looks like the rabbit is returning to his hole.

BUNNY

CUP

Here's a Bunny

Here's a bunny,
With ears so funny, (make a fist and stick up index and middle
* fingers like ears)*
And here's his hole (make a hole with other hand)
In the ground.
At the slightest
Noise he hears, (stick up fingers and wiggle)
He pricks up his ears,
Then hops to his (hop hand in front of you, then insert
* ears into the other fist)*
Hole in the ground.

- Show the children how to make a bunny with their hands, then follow along with you as you do the motions above.

Ten Little Friends

Entertain children and get their hands in their laps with Ten Little Friends.

HOW?

- Using the patterns on the next page, cut ten little faces out of felt.

- Decorate with yarn, wiggle eyes, or paint pens.

- Glue a small strip of Velcro (loop side) to the end of each inside finger of the gloves. Attach a face to each finger, then say this rhyme:

Ten Little Friends

Ten little friends went out to play (wiggle fingers in front of you)
On a very bright and sunny day.
And they had a little talk. (have fingers face each other)
Talk, talk, talk, talk, talk.
And they took a little walk. (move hands left to the right in front of you)
Walk, walk, walk, walk, walk.
'Till they came to a great big hill.
And they climbed to the top (move hands above head)
And stood very still.
'Till they all tumbled down (roll hands down to legs)
And fell to the ground.
"We're so tired," they all said. (wiggle fingers in front of you)
So they all went home
And went to bed.
1-2-3-4-5-6-7-8-9-10. (bend down fingers as you count, then place hands in lap)
Good night!

WHAT?

felt

scissors

wiggle eyes, yarn scraps, and glue gun or glue sticks; or paint pens

Velcro

pair of cloth gloves

WHAT ELSE?

You can easily do this fingerplay with or without the puppet.

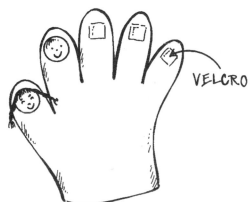

LITTLE FRIENDS

CLOTH GLOVES

VELCRO

Mr. Turkey and Mr. Duck

Let Mr. Turkey and Mr. Duck entertain busy fingers.

HOW?

• To begin this fingerplay, have the children put their hands behind their backs.

Mr. Turkey and Mr. Duck

Mr. Turkey went for a walk one day (bring out left fist with your thumb stuck up)
In the very best of weather (move fist to the beat of the words)
He met Mr. Duck along the way, (bring out right fist with thumb stuck up)
And they talked together. (have fists face each other and pretend to talk)
"Gobble, gobble, gobble." (wiggle left thumb)
"Quack, quack, quack." (wiggle right thumb)
"Good-bye." (wiggle left thumb)
"Good-bye." (wiggle right thumb)
And they both walked back.
*   (move hands behind your back)*

WHAT?

no materials needed

WHAT ELSE?

Change the names of the characters in the fingerplay. You might use storybook characters or children's names in your classroom.
For example,
Jason Jones went for a walk one day
In the very best of weather.
He met Kia Mosley along the way
And they talked together.
"Howdy, Howdy, howdy."
"Hey, hey, hey."
"Good-bye."
"Good-bye."
And they both walked away.

Mr. Alligator

Mr. Alligator will engage little hands while reinforcing language skills.

WHAT?

no materials needed

HOW?

- Tell children to make Mr. Alligator as you demonstrate by extending your arms and putting your palms together.

- Repeat the fingerplay below:

Mr. Alligator

Oh, Mr. Alligator, alligator, alligator, (open arms each time you say "alligator," increasing the volume each time)
Don't snap at me.
Oh, Mr. Alligator, alligator, alligator.
I'm not a flea.
Oh, Mr. Alligator, alligator, alligator.
I'd like a ride.
Oh, Mr. Alligator, alligator, alligator.
But not inside.
Oh, Mr. Alligator, alligator, alligator.
Please stay away.
Oh, Mr. Alligator, alligator, alligator.
It's safer that way!

WHAT ELSE?

Make a "Mr. Alligator" sock puppet to use with this rhyme. Take an old brown or green sock and glue large pom-poms to the heel of the sock. Make a ball the size of your fist out of cotton and insert it inside the sock in the heel. Put your hand in the sock and extend your fingers from your thumb to create a mouth.

Nursery Rhyme Time

Early literacy research suggests a positive correlation between children's ability to rhyme and their ability to read.

HOW?

- Below are just a few of the nursery rhymes you can use to fill bits and pieces of time during the day.

Humpty Dumpty sat on a wall,
Humpty Dumpty had a great fall.
All the king's horses,
And all the king's men,
Couldn't put Humpty together again.

Mary, Mary, quite contrary,
How does your garden grow?
With silver bells,
And cockle shells,
And pretty maids all in a row.

Jack and Jill went up the hill
To fetch a pail of water.
Jack fell down,
And broke his crown,
And Jill came tumbling after.

Hey, Diddle, Diddle, the cat and the fiddle
The cow jumped over the moon.
The little dog laughed to see such a sport.
And the dish ran away with the spoon.

Lillle Boy Blue come blow your horn.
The sheep's in the meadow,
The cow's in the corn.
Where's the little boy who looks after the sheep?
He's under the haystack, fast asleep.

WHAT?

no materials needed

WHAT ELSE?

Try singing the rhymes to the tune "100 Bottles of Beer on the Wall." Give it a try! You'll be surprised!

Animal Rhymes

Encourage children to listen and rhyme with these riddles.

WHAT?

animal patterns on
the next page

markers

scissors

Velcro (loop side)

flannel board

HOW?

- Color and cut out the farm animals.

- Attach a small piece of Velcro to the back of each one and place them on the flannel board.

- Tell the children you want them to be "detectives" and try to identify the animals in your riddles.

- Choose a child to come up and point to the animal after you read rhyme.

I give you milk.
I say, "Moo moo."
On grass and hay
I chew and chew.

"Oink, oink, oink,"
Is what I say.
In the mud
I like to play.

I like to sleep.
I also "Purrr."
I have whiskers
And very soft fur.

"Neigh, neigh,"
I gallop and run.
I'll give you a ride
That's lots of fun.

Waddle, waddle, waddle,
"Quack, quack, quack."
My feathers can be
White, yellow, or black.

"Baa, baa, baa,"
Yes, I have some wool.
"Baa, baa, baa,"
Three bags full.

"Woof, woof, woof,"
Give me a bone.
If I'm your friend
You're never alone.

I'll lay some eggs
In my nest.
"Cluck, cluck, cluck,"
I'll do my best.

WHAT ELSE?

Ask the children to identify the words that rhyme in each riddle. Let the children make up their own riddles about animals.

Have the children make different animal sounds while their friends try and guess what they are.

Let's Make Music!

Make music throughout the day to entertain children with this movement chant.

WHAT?

no materials needed

HOW?

• Sit on the floor and model what you want the children to do as you chant:

Let's Make Music

Let's make music with our hands,
Clap, clap, clap. (clap 3 times)
Let's make music with our hands,
Clap, clap, clap. (clap 3 times)
Let's make music with our hands,
Let's make music with our hands,
Let's make music with our hands,
Clap, clap, clap. (clap 3 times)

Let's make music with our fingers,
Snap, snap, snap…(snap 3 times)

Let's make music with our feet,
Tap, tap, tap…(tap feet 3 times)

We can put them all together
Clap, snap, tap…(clap, snap, and tap)

WHAT ELSE?

Ask children to suggest other ways they can make sounds with their bodies. For example, lips could smack, tongues could click, feet could stomp, and so on.

Pass out musical instruments and ask children to play them as you chant about the different instruments. For example, "Let's make music with the sticks…"

• Sing the chant to "She'll Be Comin' Around the Mountain."

Days of the Week Chant

Help children learn the days of the week with this movement chant.

HOW?

- Have the children stand and follow along with you as you say the words and make the motions.

Days of the Week Chant

Sunday, Monday, clap, clap, clap. (clap 3 times)
Tuesday, Wednesday, snap, snap, snap. (snap 3 times)
Thursday hop. (hop)
Friday stop. (hold hand up)
Saturday spin around like a top. (spin around)
Seven days are in a week. (hold up 7 fingers)
Now sit down and take a seat. (sit down quietly)

- Ask children what day of the week it is. What was yesterday? What will tomorrow be?

WHAT?

no materials needed

WHAT ELSE?

Try singing this chant to the tune of "Twinkle, Twinkle, Little Star."

Point to the words on your classroom calendar as you say them.

Print the days of the week on 2" x 4" (5 cm x 10 cm) pieces of paper and tape them to blocks. Also tape the words "Today" and "is" on blocks. Let children "build" a sentence about what day it is.

Think of adjectives to make each day special. For example: Magical Monday, Terrific Tuesday, Wonderful Wednesday, Thrilling Thursday, or Fabulous Friday.

Color Chant

This chant is an effective way to engage children in a group activity, while reinforcing color recognition and listening skills.

WHAT?

no materials needed

HOW?

• Tell the children to look at their clothes and think about what color they are wearing. Explain that they will have to listen very carefully and do what you say in the Color Chant.

Color Chant

If you're wearing RED,
Put your hands on your head.
If you're wearing BLACK,
Then touch your back.
If you're wearing BROWN,
Touch the ground.
If you're wearing GREEN,
Wash your hands real clean.
If you're wearing BLUE,
Put your hands on your shoe.
If you're wearing PINK,
Then think and think.
If you're wearing GRAY,
Have a nice day.

IF ORANGE is what you wear,
Then touch your hair.
If you're wearing WHITE,
Squeeze your hands real tight.
If you're wearing PURPLE,
Say, "Murple gurple."
If you're wearing YELLOW,
Wave to your fellow.
You're all looking mighty fine,
And that's the end of the color
*   rhyme!*

The Shape Family

This chant will help children remember shapes.

HOW?

- Cut shapes out of felt using the patterns on the following page. (Glue on facial features cut from felt scraps if you desire.)

- Place the shapes on the flannel board and point to them as you chant the verse below:

  The Shape Family
  I am momma circle, round like a pie.
  I'm baby triangle, three sides have I.
  I'm papa square, my sides are four.
  I'm cool cousin rectangle, shaped like a door.
  I am sister oval, shaped like a zero.
  We are the shapes that you all know.
  Look for us wherever you go.

- Sing the chant to "I'm a Little Teapot."

WHAT?

felt scraps

shape patterns on the following page

scissors

flannel board

WHAT ELSE?

Have children identify objects in the classroom that are shaped like the characters in the chant. You might say, "Who can find something in the room with three sides like baby triangle?"

Play "I Spy" with shapes. For example, "I spy something that is shaped like sister oval."

Ask the children to close their eyes. Remove one of the shapes. Can they identify the missing shape?

Cut geometric shapes out of construction paper and give one to each child to hold. Ask the children to hold up their shapes as they are mentioned in the chant.

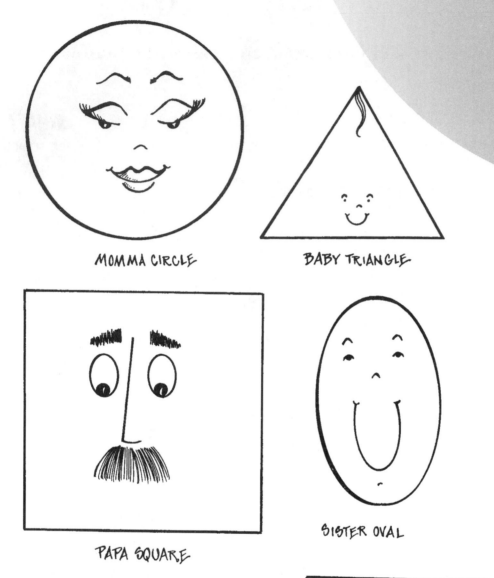

MOMMA CIRCLE

BABY TRIANGLE

PAPA SQUARE

SISTER OVAL

COOL COUSIN RECTANGLE

Alphabet Chant

Try this chant to line up for play time or to move to another activity in the school.

HOW?

- Begin marching and slapping your arms on your sides as you say the chant below.

Alphabet Chant (Children repeat each line.)

A B C D E F G
A B C D E F G
School is so much fun to me.
School is so much fun to me.
H I J K L M N
H I J K L M N
Learn and play with all my friends.
Learn and play with all my friends.
O P Q R S and T
O P Q R S and T
We're the best as you can see.
We're the best as you can see.
U V W X Y Z
U V W X Y Z
Now it's time to stop and FREEZE!
Now it's time to stop and FREEZE!

- When children freeze, quietly give them directions or motion for them to follow you.

WHAT?

no materials needed

WHAT ELSE?

Change the last words of the chant to say, "Now, look at your teacher, please"; "Now walk quietly, please"; "Now get on your coats, please"; or whatever else you want them to do.

Granny at the Fair

This chant is great for releasing wiggles and developing auditory memory skills.

WHAT?

no materials needed

HOW?

• Simply begin saying this chant and the children will join in:

Granny went to the county fair,
And she brought back a rocking chair.
And she rocked, and she rocked, (rock back and forth)
And she rocked, and she rocked.
Granny went to the county fair, (continue rocking)
And she got a fan while she was there.
And she fanned, and she fanned, (fan with left hand)
And she fanned, and she fanned,
And she rocked, and she rocked,
And she rocked, and she rocked.

• Add these verses and motions to "Granny went to the county fair":

And she got some scissors while she was there.
And she cut... (cut with right hand)
And she fanned...and she rocked...

• End with:

And she got some gum while she was there.
And she chewed...and she cut...(pretend to chew)
And she fanned...and she rocked...
And she blew a bubble while she was there.
And she blew, and she blew, (put hands by mouth and extend
  as if blowing a bubble)
And she blew, and POP! (clap on "POP!")

WHAT ELSE?

After several repetitions of this chant, begin changing the ending to keep their interest and increase their anticipation. Blow longer, make the bubble bigger, change your speed, etc.

Cool Bear Hunt

How about going on a Cool Bear Hunt for a break during the day? And just think of all the skills children are developing as they have fun—motor, auditory memory, sequence, language, imagination, positional words, and so much more!

HOW?

• Begin this chant by acting out the motions as you tell the children to get out their backpacks and open them up. Say, "Let's put in some crackers in case we get hungry. And let's put in a thermos of milk in case we get thirsty. Oh, and put in a flashlight in case it's dark. Okay, zip them up, put them on your backs, stand up, and repeat after me."

WHAT?

no materials needed

The Cool Bear Hunt (children repeat each line)
Chorus:
We're going on a bear hunt. (slap thighs)
We're going to catch a big one. (stretch out arms)
With big, green eyes, (make circles around eyes with hands)
And a fuzzy, little tail. (put hands behind back to make a tail)

Look over there. (point to the right)
It's a candy factory.
Can't go over it. (put hands over head)
Can't go under it. (put hands down low)
Can't go around it. (circle arms in front of you)
Guess we'll go through it. (shrug, then point forward)
Mmmmmmm! (pretend to gobble up candy)

Chorus

Look over there. (point to the left)
It's a peanut butter river. (make appropriate motions)
Can't go over it.
Can't go under it.
Can't go around it.
Guess we'll go through it.
Uh-uh-uh-uh. (pretend to swim slowly)
Hey, let's get out the crackers. (pretend to dip cracker in peanut butter)

And the thermos of milk. (take top off thermos)
Glug, glug, glug. (hold to mouth)
Ah! (wipe hand across mouth)

Chorus

Look over there. (point in front of you)
It's a Jell-O swamp.
Can't go over it. (make appropriate motions)
Can't go under it.
Can't go around it.
Guess we'll go through it.
Glub, glub, glub. (wiggle and jiggle all over)

Chorus

Look over there. (point behind you)
It's a cave.
Can't go over it. (make appropriate motions)
Can't go under it.
Can't go around it.
Guess we'll go through it.
Let's get out our flashlights. (pretend to hold flashlight)
It's cold in here. (shiver)
I see two big, green eyes.
And a fuzzy, little tail.
IT'S A BEAR! (throw arms in air)
Go through the Jell-O swamp.
Glub, glub, glub. (wiggle and jiggle)
Swim across the peanut butter river.
Uh-uh-uh-uh. (swim arms)
Go through the candy factory.
Mmmmmm! (pretend to gobble)
Go home.
Open the door. (pretend to open door)
Shut the door. (close the door)
Sit down. (sit down on the floor)
Whew! (wipe forehead)
We went on a bear hunt. (slap thighs)
And we weren't afraid! (shake heads)

CHAPTER 7

A Story for Your Pocket

With a story in your pocket, you'll be able to transition from one activity to another or one time of the day to another *and* spark children's imaginations and develop their language skills. In this chapter you'll find a tell-and-draw story, a paper cut story, a file folder story, a flannel board story, and participation stories, as well as ideas for books in which children can create their own stories. These simple tales are sure to bring out the storyteller in each of you. And don't be surprised if you hear your children say, "Tell it again!"

Scout—A Tell-and-Draw Story

This tell-and-draw story will entertain children whenever you have a few extra minutes.

WHAT?

large sheet of paper

marker

HOW?

• Tell the story as you draw the illustrations on the paper.

One day I was walking in the park looking for my best friend when I accidentally stepped in a beehive.

The bees came out and swarmed all over me.

So I jumped in a pond of water, but they would not go away.

I saw a big hill, so I ran up it.

There were two doors with doorknobs that I tried to open, but they were locked.

So I ran down one side of the hill.

Then I ran down the other side of the hill.

And I finally found my best friend—my dog SCOUT! He scared those bees away and licked my face.

WHAT ELSE?

Repeat the story, pausing and asking the children to tell what happens next. Older children will enjoy trying to draw and tell the story themselves.

Use a chalkboard, dry erase board, or overhead projector for telling this tale.

Tilly the Flying Fish

Children will be delighted with this story about the little fish that wanted to fly. They'll enjoy retelling the story with their own little paper fish.

HOW?

- Cut out a paper fish for each child using the pattern on this page.

- Give one to each child and show them how to hook the tabs together to make a fish.

- Tell them to put their fingers in their fish and swim it around as you tell the story below:

Once there was a little fish named Tilly. Every day Tilly would swim along the ocean floor and dream of what it would be like to go above the water. She asked her mother if she could fly above the ocean, just to take a peek at the world above, but her mother only laughed and said, "Who ever heard of a flying fish!"

One day as Tilly was swimming along she ran into a giant octopus who was tangled up in some coral and rocks on the ocean floor. "Help! Help!" screamed the octopus. Now, any ordinary little fish would have been scared and swam away, but not little Tilly. She bravely started untangling the octopus' arms until the octopus was free at last. Lucky for Tilly it was a magic octopus and it gave Tilly one wish to thank her. Tilly thought for a minute, and then she said, "I wish, I wish that I could fly."

And do you know what she did then? That's right! She swam to the top of the water and she jumped in the air and she FLEW! **(Have the children stand up, toss their fish in the air, and watch them fly.)**

WHAT?

paper

scissors

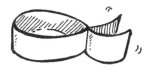

Baby Bird

This story is especially fun to tell in the spring when you notice real birds building nests.

WHAT?

construction paper

scissors

marker

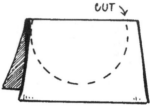

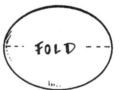

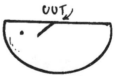

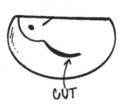

HOW?

• Have the paper, scissors, and marker in your lap as you begin telling the story below. Cut the paper according to the directions.

It was spring and time for the birds to build a nest. What do you think the birds used to build their nest? (Accept all answers from the children.) Did you know that birds are natural recyclers because they take bits of string, trash, hair, and other things people throw away and use them to build their nests? The birds worked very hard carrying things in their little beaks and built a nest that looked like this. (Fold the paper in half and cut out a semi-circle on the fold.)

Mother bird sat on her nest a long time, and she laid a beautiful egg. (Open the paper to reveal the egg.)

She had to sit on the egg in the sun and in the rain. She couldn't leave her precious, little egg. She would have been very lonesome, but she made friends with two little bugs. This is what they looked like. (Draw dots on either side of the nest.)

They came to talk to the mother bird every day.

One day the mother bird heard a little sound. She looked down and there was a small crack in the egg. (Cut a slit toward the dots.)

Then she heard a big cracking sound. (Cut a line around the dots, then slant toward the outside as shown.)

And what do you think came out of that crack? You're right! It was a baby bird! (Open the egg, bend up the beak, and fold back the edge to create a bird.)

Monkey's Mischief

Children love to hear about others getting into mischief. When you repeat this story, children will feel confident as they predict what will happen next. The alliteration of the chant will also enhance phonemic awareness.

HOW?

- Color the picture of the monkey's cage on page 149.

- Glue it to the front of the file folder.

- Cut out the shape of the monkey from file folder and paper at the same time.

- Cut the construction paper into 8" x 10" (20 cm x 25 cm) rectangles and insert them inside the file folder in the following order: brown, blue, red, yellow, green, brown.

- Tape the sides of the file folder together.

- Glue a copy of the story that follows on the back of the file folder so you can hold it up and read it as the children watch the monkey change colors. Encourage the children to join in on the chorus.

WHAT?

copy of monkey's cage (see illustration on page 149)

crayons

file folder

glue

scissors

construction paper (brown, blue, red, yellow, green, brown)

tape

Monkey's Mischief

Once there was a little monkey who lived at the zoo with all the other monkeys. He'd swing from the ropes in his cage, eat bananas, and chatter with his monkey friends. But somehow he just always seemed to be getting into mischief!

One day some painters were painting the inside of the zoo. They left some cans of paint open that night when they went home. After the other animals had gone to sleep, the little monkey stuck his tail through the bars of his cage and dipped his tail into some blue paint. He used his tail like a paintbrush and painted himself all blue. **(Remove the brown sheet of paper to reveal the blue paper.)** *Can you imagine what the children thought when they arrived at the zoo the next morning and saw blue monkey? They all said:*

Chorus:
Ha, ha, ha.
Chee, chee, chee.
What a silly
Monkey is he!

The next night the painters once again left out some paint. This time the little monkey dipped his tail in the red paint and painted himself all red. **(Remove the blue sheet of paper to reveal red.)** The next day when the children arrived at the zoo they all laughed and said:

Chorus

When the painters left that night, the monkey put his tail in the yellow paint and painted himself all yellow. **(Remove the red sheet of paper.)** The children all laughed the next day and said:

Chorus

On the following night, guess what the monkey did again? That's right. This time he dipped his tail in green paint. **(Remove the yellow paper.)** The children giggled when they saw him and said:

Chorus

Although the boys and girls laughed at the little monkey each day, the other monkeys would have nothing to do with him. "Who ever heard of a red or blue or yellow or green monkey?" they would say. Little monkey was very sad and lonely, so that night he decided to paint himself brown again. **(Remove the green paper.)** All the other monkeys were so glad to have him back as a friend, they had a special party and ate bunches and bunches of bananas. Little monkey only smiled and said, "No more monkey business for me! From now on I'll just be myself!"

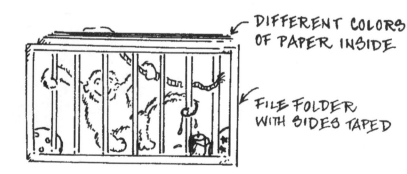

DIFFERENT COLORS OF PAPER INSIDE

FILE FOLDER WITH SIDES TAPED

Lucky's Surprise!

The repetition and pattern in this story will appeal to children, and the different versions will enable you to adapt it throughout the school year.

WHAT?

orange sheet of
construction paper

scissors

HOW?

• Have the orange paper and scissors in your lap as you begin telling the story on the next page.

Lucky's Halloween Surprise!

It was that time of year when the leaves changed colors and the air was crisp. The chipmunk family had been busy storing up food for the long, cold winter, and they were ready for a celebration. Lucy Chipmunk said to her husband, Lucky, "Why don't you go over to the pumpkin patch and get a pumpkin? We'll invite all our friends and have a Halloween party."

So Lucky took his big scissors and headed through the woods and over the field to the pumpkin patch. He looked around and around until he found an enormous pumpkin. He cut it off the vine with his scissors and very slowly dragged it across the field and through the woods back to their home at the foot of the old oak tree. (Fold the paper in half. Cut up from the fold to make a stem and half a pumpkin as indicated on the pattern.) Lucky called, "Lucy, come and see the enormous pumpkin I found." (Open up the paper to show the pumpkin.) Lucy went out to look and said, "Lucky, that's a mighty pretty pumpkin, but you know that's too big to fit in our little house. Now go back and find another pumpkin that's smaller."

So Lucky started back through the woods and across the field until he came to the pumpkin patch. He looked around and around until he found another pumpkin...

• (The story continues as Lucky keeps dragging home pumpkins that are too large. Each time he finds a pumpkin, cut in from the original shape ½". Let the previous outline fall to the ground. When there is just a tiny pumpkin left, end the story...)

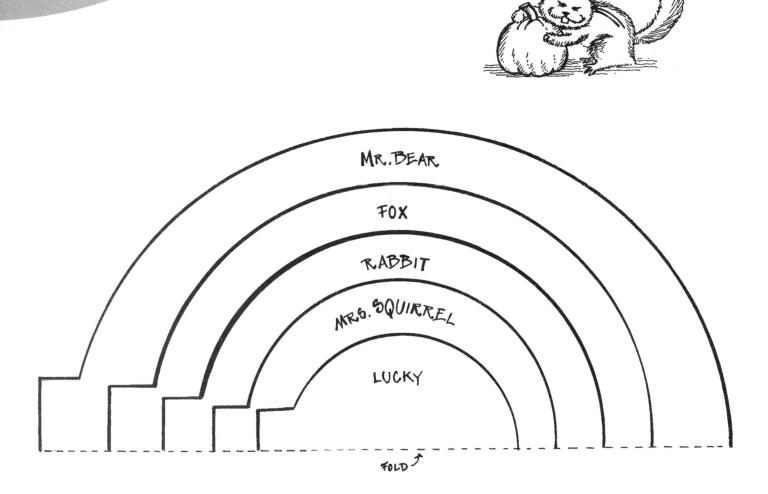

*Lucky dragged that tiny pumpkin across the field and through the woods until he got back to their home. Lucky called, "Lucy, come see the tiny pumpkin I found." Lucy said, "Why, Lucky, that's just the right size. But what are we going to do with all these other pumpkins?" By then the other animals in the forest had gathered around to see what was going on. Lucky looked at all the pumpkins, then he looked at his friends. Lucky got a big smile on his face as he handed one to Mr. Bear, one to the fox, one to the rabbit, and one to Mrs. Squirrel. **(Pick the scraps off the floor, open them up, and hand them to children in the class.)** The animals carved their pumpkins into jack-o-lanterns. Then they had a wonderful Halloween party together.*

WHAT ELSE?

Vary the story for different holidays and seasons.

Winter:
white paper, cut-out snowman

Valentine's Day:
red paper, cut-out heart

Thanksgiving:
orange paper, cut-out pumpkin

Spring:
blue paper, cut-out kite

Summer:
green paper, cut-out watermelon

WINTER (SNOWMAN)

VALENTINE'S DAY

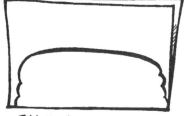

THANKSGIVING (PUMPKIN)

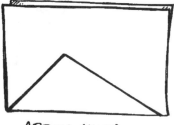

SPRING (KITE)

SUMMER (WATERMELON)

The Story of Chicken Little

Give children the opportunity to "perform" with this folk tale.

HOW?

- Print the names of the characters listed below on the index cards.

> Chicken Little
> Ducky Lucky
> Henny Penny
> Turkey Lurky
> Goosey Loosey
> Foxy Loxy
> The King

- Punch two holes at the top of each card, then tie on a piece of string, large enough to fit over a child's head.

- Choose the characters for the story and have the children put on their nametags and spread out around the room.

- Place the acorn in the sack, then gather it at the top.

- Stand near Chicken Little with the sack in your hand and begin telling the story. Walk through the story the first time, guiding children and having them repeat their lines.

> *Once there was a little chicken named "Chicken Little." One day as she was playing outside something fell on her head. She picked it up, put it in her bag and said, "The sky is falling. I must go and tell the King."* **(Hand the bag with the acorn to Chicken Little.)** *Chicken Little went on down the road until she met her friend Ducky Lucky*. **(Walk Chicken Little over to where Ducky Lucky is standing.)** *Ducky Lucky said, "Where are you going in such a hurry?" "The sky is falling. I must go and tell the King," replied Chicken Little. Ducky Lucky said, "May I go with you?" Chicken Little said, "Please do."*
>
> *Chicken Little and Ducky Lucky went on down the road until they met Henny Penny.* **(Walk the Chicken Little and Ducky Lucky to Henny Penny.)** *Henny Penny asked, "Where are you going?" "The sky is falling. We are on our way to tell the King."*

WHAT?

large index cards or
heavy paper

markers

hole punch

string

large paper grocery
sack

acorn or similar nut

WHAT ELSE?

Retell the story many times, choosing different children to be the characters.

Ask children to think of different endings for the story, then act out their versions.

"May I go with you?" asked Henny Penny. "Please do," answered Chicken Little and Ducky Lucky.

The story continues as they meet Turkey Lurkey, Goosey Loosey, and Foxy Loxy.

When the animals finally arrived at the King's palace, the King asked, "What are you doing?" The animals all said, "The sky is falling!" "How do you know?" asked the King. "It fell on my head," replied Chicken Little. "Here it is," said Chicken Little and she handed her bag to the King. The King looked in the bag, and started laughing. "Oh, Chicken Little, it's only an acorn that fell on your head! It's not the sky at all!"

• End the story by having the children tell what lesson they think Chicken Little and the other animals learned.

The Case of the Missing Shoe

Use this story to reinforce colors, rhymes, and auditory skills.

HOW?

- Cut two shoes out of each color of felt using the pattern above.

- Place one blue shoe on the felt board to begin the story.

- Add shoes of different colors as indicated in the story.

It's time for school. What will I do? (blue shoe)
Please help me look for my missing shoe! (leave this shoe up on the board)
Let's look by that box of Jell-O. (yellow shoe)
Oh, it's only a shoe of ____. (children supply the missing word)
Maybe it's in the washing machine. (green shoe)
Oh, it's only a shoe of ____.
I bet the shoe is under my bed. (red shoe)
Oh, it's just a shoe of ____.
I know. It's under the bathroom sink. (pink shoe)
Oh, it's only a shoe of ____.
Maybe it's by my bowl of porridge. (orange shoe)
Oh, it's only a shoe of ____.
Perhaps it's by the maple syrple. (purple shoe)
Oh, it's only a shoe of ____.
I'll look by my brand new light. (white shoe)
Oh, it's only a shoe of ____.
It might be by my stuffed clown. (brown shoe)
Oh, it's only a shoe of ____.
I know, it's in my back pack. (black shoe)
Oh, it's only a shoe of ____.
Where, oh where could my other shoe be? (blue shoe)
Well, it's on my foot. Silly me! (put up matching blue shoe)

WHAT?

scrap pieces of felt (blue, brown, red, green, orange, yellow, white, black, purple, pink)

scissors

felt board

zip baggie

WHAT ELSE?

Use the shoes for a visual matching game. Hide one shoe of each color around the room in plain sight. Pass out the other shoes to the children. The children walk around the room and hunt for their matching shoe.

Animal Cookies

Animal cookies are a favorite of children, and this poem will be, too.

WHAT?

box of animal cookies

felt scraps

scissors

glue

flannel board

HOW?

• First, eat the animal cookies!

• Cut out felt "animal cookies" using the patterns on the opposite page.

• Glue the poem below to the back of the box, and put the felt animals inside.

• Pull the animals out of the box and place them on the flannel board as you read the rhyme.

Animal crackers
In my box
Open the lid,
And out they'll pop.
First comes elephant
Swinging his trunk.
He moves very slowly,
Thump, thump, thump.
Silly monkey
Jumps up and down.
He eats bananas
And swings around.
Tall giraffe
Wrinkles his nose.
He has spots
From head to toe.
Lion growls
And paces around.
He's the king
Of jungle ground.
Humpback camel
Blinks his eyes
And looks about
With great surprise.

Hippo dives
In the water deep.
He eats some grass
And then he sleeps.
Catch them quick!
They're on the run.
Eat them up.
Yum! Yum! Yum!

WHAT ELSE?

Let the children dramatize the poem and pretend to be the different animals as you read it.

Have the children pull an animal out of the box and move like that animal to their next activity.

Use real animal cookies as you recite the poem, then pass them out for snack.

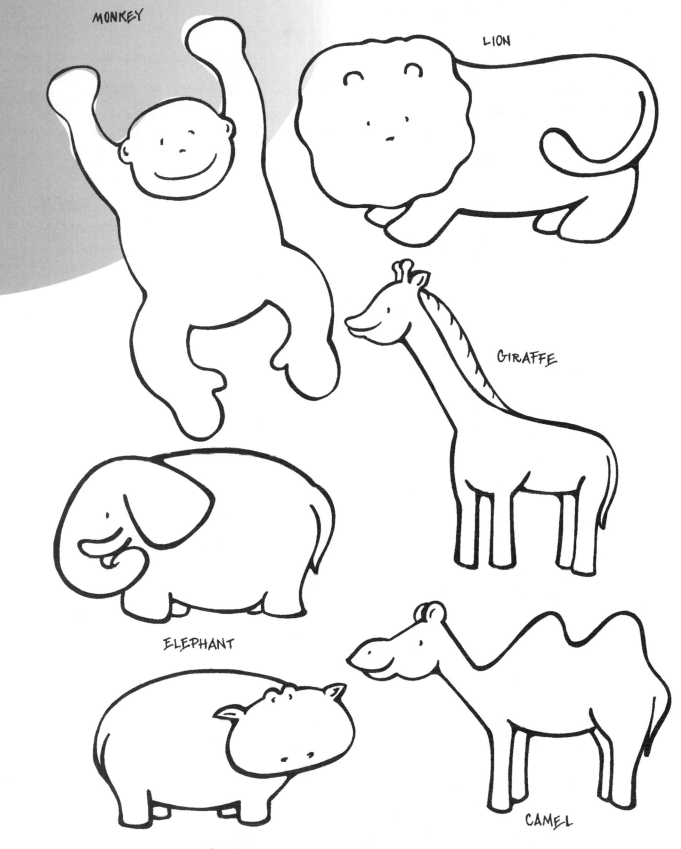

MONKEY

LION

GIRAFFE

ELEPHANT

HIPPO

CAMEL

Felt Fun

Children can use this individual activity at rest time or with a friend to develop language skills and their imaginations.

WHAT?

file folder

stapler

9" x 12"
(22.5 cm x 30 cm)
piece of felt

glue

felt scraps

scissors

HOW?

• Make an individual felt board by stapling the sides of the file folder together.

• Glue the felt piece to the front of the file folder.

• Cut out your own felt pieces or use the patterns on pages 133 and 157 to make felt characters.

• Place the felt pieces inside the file folder. Demonstrate how to take the characters out of the folder and make up stories with them.

• Let children suggest other stories that could be told with the felt pieces.

• Place the felt folder in the classroom library or use to help a child settle down for rest. It could also be used to redirect a child who needs a quiet activity to calm down.

WHAT ELSE?

Make several of the felt folders to hold other flannel board stories, such as the "Gingerbread Boy," "Little Red Hen," "Three Pigs," and so on.

Turn an old picture frame into a flannel board. Remove the glass. Glue felt to the cardboard backing in the frame. Use the stand on the back of the frame to prop it up.

STORE PIECES INSIDE

1. STAPLE SIDES TOGETHER

2. GLUE FELT DOWN

3. ADD TO THE FRONT FOR THE STORY

One-Minute Dramas

Enhance children's imaginations and creativity with these one-minute dramas.

HOW?

• Dip the end of the stick or cardboard roller in glue, then roll it in glitter to make a magic wand.

• Explain to the children that you will describe a scene. When you wave your magic wand over them, they will become part of the scene.

• Make up short scenarios similar to the following.

Going on a picnic
Caterpillars turning into butterflies
Autumn leaves falling down
Ducklings hatching from eggs
Merry-go-round horses moving up and down
A birthday party
Popcorn popping
Ice-skaters
Riding a bicycle
Being a clown in the circus
Dogs fetching a bone
Flowers growing
Astronauts in space
Pancakes cooking
Robots in the future
Taking a bath
Eating juicy watermelon
Making a snowman
Getting lost in a store
Riding a magic carpet

WHAT?

wooden chopsticks, cardboard roller from a pants hanger, or wooden dowel

glue

glitter

Imagination Story

Here's another open-ended activity to challenge children's imaginations.

WHAT?

no materials needed

HOW?

• Open up your hands to look like a book.

• Ask the children to do the same as you say the chant below:

Here is my imagination book.
Open the pages and take a look.

• Make up a sentence about what you see in your book. For example, "I see a squirrel and he's running up a tree to hide his nuts."

• Call on children one at a time and encourage them to make up a sentence about what they see in their "pretend" book.

WHAT ELSE?

After children feel comfortable with this activity, use it to tell group stories. Ask all the children to get out their "imagination books" and explain that you will begin a story. As you go around the group, they will all get to add to the story. For example, "Once upon a time in a faraway land, there lived a beautiful princess...." When all the children have contributed to the story, bring closure to it with a happy ending.

Use this strategy for problem solving with the children. Open your book and describe a stressful situation. Have the children brainstorm what they would do. For example, "In my book I see a child who is going to cross a busy street. What should the child do?" or "In my book I see a child who is home alone. Somebody comes to the door and knocks. What should the child do?"

Story Cape

Set the stage for an exciting story or good book by putting on this cape.

HOW?

- Sew a 1" (2.5 cm) casing at the top of the fabric. Hem the bottom edge.

- Cut a 16" (40 cm) piece of elastic.

- Thread the elastic through the casing, gathering the fabric as you do so.

- Sew the ends of the elastic in place.

- Sew Velcro to each end of the cape so it can be fastened around the neck.

- Before reading a book or telling a story, put on the cape to get the children's attention.

WHAT?

1 yard (1 meter) of fabric

needle and thread

¾" (2 cm) wide elastic

scissors

1" (2.5 cm) piece of Velcro

ELASTIC

HEM

SEW ENDS CLOSED TO HOLD ELASTIC

VELCRO

WHAT ELSE?

Let the children take turns wearing the story cape as they read a book or tell a story to their friends.

Make capes out of different fabrics for the children to wear when they act out stories. Black is perfect for witches and monsters, red is good for Little Red Riding Hood, and gold or silver lame works well for kings and queens.

The Picnic Book

Turn your children into authors and illustrators by teaching them how to make these little books.

WHAT?

plain paper

crayons

pens

colored pencils

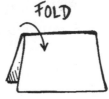

FOLD

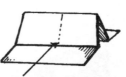

TEAR TO HERE

HOW?

- Demonstrate how to make a book by telling the story below.

- After you do it several times, the children will want to make their own. (The story will give them an easy way to remember and associate the steps.)

> Let's go on a picnic.
> We'll need a picnic basket. **(Fold the paper in half.)**
> Let's take hotdogs. **(Fold the paper in fourths.)**
> Let's take hamburgers. **(Fold the paper in eighths.)**
> Here's a picnic bench. **(Open the paper so it's folded in half. Fold one side to the top, fold the other side to the top.)**
> Let's share it with a friend. **(Fold down half way on the crease.)**
> All we need now is a book **(Bend down as shown.)**
> To draw pictures of our good time. **(Wrap pages around to make a book.)**

WHAT ELSE?

Use different colors of paper to make these books.

Give children stickers, rubber stamps, and other art media to create with.

Mini-Libraries

Children will be motivated to write and read their own books with their mini-libraries. Creating the books will keep them busy, and reading their books can entertain them at rest time or other transitional times in your day.

HOW?

• Give each child a small cereal box. Demonstrate how to cut off the top flaps.

• Offer them some of the materials suggested to use in decorating their boxes.

• Make sure they put their name on their "library."

• Explain that when they make little books, they can collect them in their own libraries.

• Have them keep their libraries in their desks or cubbies, and remind them to get them out during independent reading time or at rest time.

WHAT?

individual cereal boxes

scrap wrapping paper

wallpaper

contact paper

art supplies

WHAT ELSE?

Encourage the children to exchange books with their friends.

Children can make books relating to classroom concepts, such as number books, shape books, letter books, word families, themes, or seasons. They could make books about their families, things they like, pets, and other personal interests. These books could also be used for retelling stories or as a follow-up to class experiences, such as a field trip or party.

Zip It Up!

Class books give children the opportunity to develop reading and writing skills.

WHAT?

paper

scissors

large zipper bags

crayons

stapler

duct tape

HOW?

• Give each child a sheet of paper that has been cut to fit in the bag.

• Ask them to draw a picture of themselves on the paper doing something they do well.

• Write each child's ending to this sentence on the paper. "(Child's name) can _____."

• Place the child's picture in each bag, then zip shut. Lay the bags on top of each other and staple them together. Cover the staples with duct tape.

• When you have a few extra minutes, show the book as you read each child's sentence.

WHAT ELSE?

Make several books similar to the one above around classroom themes, field trips, books read, holidays, and topics suggested below.

Things I Love

I Like to Eat

If I Could Make a Wish

My Favorite Animal

Feelings

Friends

My Favorite Book

Store class-made books in a basket and pull them out for children to look at during "in-between" times.

Story Web

Visual graphics enable children to grasp the whole, as well as the parts of a story or concept. It's also a wonderful technique for developing recall and comprehension skills.

HOW?

• Following a story, draw a web similar to the one below on a piece of paper or dry erase board. Put the title of the story in the middle, then encourage the children to recall the different elements as you write them on the web.

WHAT?

large sheet of paper or dry erase board

markers

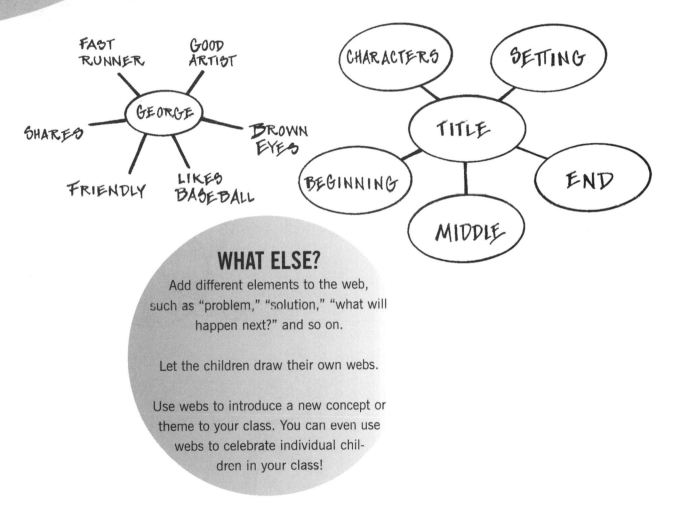

WHAT ELSE?

Add different elements to the web, such as "problem," "solution," "what will happen next?" and so on.

Let the children draw their own webs.

Use webs to introduce a new concept or theme to your class. You can even use webs to celebrate individual children in your class!

CHAPTER 8

Tricks for Any Time!

This chapter is a treasure box of "tricks" to help children learn what behavior is expected of them and strategies to keep your classroom running smoothly throughout the day. There are props to boost learning, class cheers and celebrations, and practical solutions to everyday problems.

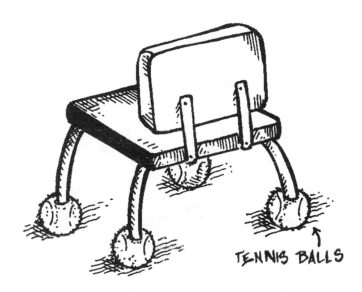

TENNIS BALLS

Eye Can

Support children when they try new things, and nurture their self-confidence with this clever prop.

WHAT?

cardboard can from chips or a drink mix

construction paper

scissors

glue

old magazines

HOW?

• Cover the outside of the can with construction paper.

• Cut eyes out of magazines and glue them all around the can.

• Explain to the children the importance of believing in yourself and trying. Ask children to give examples of when they didn't think they could do something, but they tried and they could do it.

• Show them the can and tell them if you hear them say, "I can't," you'll give them the Eye Can to remind them that they can if they try.

• If a child expresses self-doubt or says, "I can't do it," hand him the can and say, "I can."

WHAT ELSE?

Encourage the children to give the can to friends when they need it.

Use wiggly eyes to make a similar can.

Let each child decorate their own Eye Can, and write things they can do on strips of paper and store them in the can.

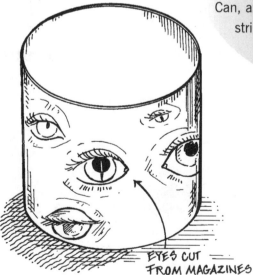

EYES CUT FROM MAGAZINES

Mr. Good for You

Encourage children and recognize their efforts with this prop.

HOW?

- To make a "Good for You" hand, draw a face on the palm of the glove similar to the one in the illustration.

- Stuff the glove with cotton or plastic grocery bags cut in strips.

- Gather the glove at the bottom and tie with a ribbon.

- Introduce the glove as "Mr. Good for You." Walk around the room and pat each child on the back and say something positive about them. Explain that Mr. Good for You is going to stay on the shelf, but when they do something special they can get him and give themselves a pat on the back.

- When you notice children accomplishing a new task, helping a friend, or working hard, tell them to, "Get Mr. Good for You and give yourself a pat on your back!"

WHAT?

cloth glove

markers

cotton stuffing or strips of plastic grocery bags

piece of ribbon, approximately 12" (30 cm)

HINT!

When patting yourself on the back, demonstrate how to take your right hand, cross over your body, and pat yourself on the left side of your back.

PAT ON THE BACK

Relax Bottle

This bottle may help children relax, focus, and calm down. (This is a much more positive alternative to time out and is more effective.)

WHAT?

plastic bottle

crayon shavings

water

glue gun or super glue

HOW?

- Remove the label from the bottle.

- Put several spoonfuls of crayon shavings in the bottle, then fill with water.

- Glue on the lid with a glue gun or super glue.

- If a child is out of control, shake up the bottle and then hand it to the child. Ask him to hold the bottle until all the crayons have stopped moving around.

LID GLUED ON

SWIRLING WATER

CRAYON SHAVINGS

WHAT ELSE?

You can also play Beat the Bottle. Shake up the bottle, and challenge the children to be sitting on the floor with their eyes on you before everything in the bottle stops moving around.

Positive Feedback

Use this "trick" as a positive behavior cue.

HOW?

- Pour ½ cup (125 ml) of corn syrup in the bottle.

- Add 1 teaspoon (5 ml) of glitter or seasonal confetti to the bottle, a drop of food coloring, and glue on the lid.

- As you're waiting to begin an activity, hand the bottle to the child who is modeling appropriate behavior and say, "You are doing the right thing."

- Continue doing this throughout the day to reinforce positive behavior.

WHAT?

plastic bottle

clear corn syrup

measuring cup

teaspoon

glitter or seasonal confetti

food coloring

gluc gun

WHAT ELSE?

Change props every week. For example, you might use a stuffed animal, a squeeze ball, a puppet, or a small action figure.

Fill a bottle with mineral oil and then add confetti, beads, or small trinkets.

HINT!

Make sure you recognize all children's attempts and try to give everyone a turn.

Me and the Music

Listening to music can help relax children,
as well as improve their cognitive abilities.
A personal cassette player can be offered to children who are
stressed or are having trouble focusing.

WHAT?

personal cassette
player

classical music tapes

HOW?

- Ask the children if they like to listen to music. What kinds of music do they like? What kind of music helps them relax or think?

- Explain that you have classical music cassettes that they can listen to on the cassette player if they want to be alone or think better.

- Offer this to a child who seems upset, then talk about how it affected them.

WHAT ELSE?

Experiment with different
types of music for different tasks in
the classroom.

Children might experiment with music
in the art center, while they do
math, as they read, when they
rest, and so forth.

Peaceful Spray

Certain aromas have different effects on the brain and body.
Lavender or rosemary tends to have a calming affect
on behavior, so try this technique on rainy days or
when tempers start to flare.

HOW?

- When children are acting stressful or aggressive, tell the children that you have some Peaceful Spray to make them feel better.
- Spray the lavender around the room.
- Ask children how it makes them feel.

WHAT?

lavender air spray

WHAT ELSE?

You can make your own Peaceful Spray by adding a few drops of lavender oil or dried rosemary to a spray bottle of water. (Some children are allergic to lavender or other scents, so substitute dried rosemary to calm behavior.)

Using a nail, punch small holes in a plastic bottle. Fill with lavender potpourri.

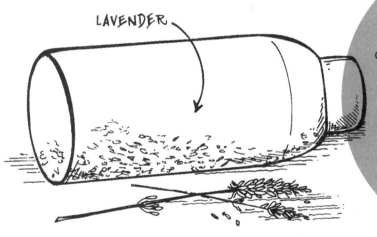

LAVENDER

Peace Talks

If children are fighting, this technique helps them express their thoughts and work toward mediation.

WHAT?

spiral notebook or large sheet of newsprint

crayons

pencils

HOW?

• Write "Peace Talks" on the notebook.

• If children are having an argument, ask them to sit at a table next to each other.

• Open up the book and say, "You draw what happened on this side" to the child on the right and "You draw what happened here," to the child on the left.

• As children draw their versions of the incident, they will begin to verbalize their thoughts.

• Many times they will resolve their own problems, or you may have to mediate by asking each child to discuss his picture and describe his point of view. Ask, "What do you think you can do about it?"

WHAT ELSE?

Older children could write their explanation of what happened.

Have children sit cross-legged on the floor, hold hands, and discuss what occurred. Eye contact and the sense of touch will often resolve conflicts.

Problem Solver

Turn children who continually complain about other children into problem solvers, and you will distract them as you empower them to resolve their own conflicts.

HOW?

- Explain to the children that many times they come to you to report situations when they could solve their own problems.

- To help you, you are going to let them take turns being the Problem Solver, and people can go to them instead of you with minor problems. (You do need to emphasize they should come to you with emergencies. Let them give examples of situations that are emergencies and those that are not.)

- Choose the child that complains the most to be the first Problem Solver.

- When children come to you, ask them if they've been to the Problem Solver first.

WHAT?

no materials needed

WHAT ELSE?

At the end of the day, ask the Problem Solver to share some of the concerns friends had and how they solved the problems. Encourage other children to suggest other alternatives.

Make a badge for the Problem Solver to wear.

Use the Problem Solver as a permanent classroom job so all children can have a turn to try and resolve problems.

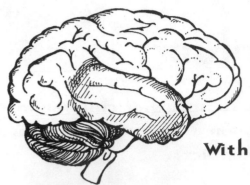

Thank Your Brain

With young children, it's not important that they get the "right" answer. We want them to THINK! Make them aware of their "brain power" with this idea.

WHAT?

no materials needed

HOW?

• When you ask children questions, rather than judging their answer or telling them it's "right" or "wrong," say, "Good thinking! Thank your brain!" (Demonstrate how to do this by patting the top of your head.)

WHAT ELSE?

Avoid questions that have a "yes" or "no" answer. Instead use open-ended questions similar to those below:

What do you think would happen if…?

Why?

Who else thinks they know?

Explain your thinking…?

What would you do if…?

How are ____ and _____ alike?

How are they different?

The answer is _____. What is the question?

What question would you like to ask me?

Masking Tape Message

This is a special way to recognize important events in children's lives. It will also help other school personnel understand the children's excitement.

HOW?

• When a child has a grandparent coming to visit, has a new sibling, just learned how to jump rope, or some other exciting event, write about it on the masking tape and tape it on their shirt.

• They will be proud, and others will be able to acknowledge it.

WHAT?

wide masking tape

markers

I HAVE A NEW BABY SISTER!

WE'RE MOVING

HINT!
Follow the child's lead with this activity. If they think something is important, then give credibility to it. Always ask them if they would like to wear the message.

WHAT ELSE?

Staple a few pieces of paper together. Ask the child to draw or write on the first page, which will be the cover for the book. Write, draw, or ask the child to dictate information about events that are important to the child. Record events throughout the year, and send the book home with the child at the end of the year.

Tooth Fairy Necklace

Here's an idea to celebrate that special moment when a child loses a tooth. It will also keep the tooth from getting lost.

WHAT?

film containers

large nail

hammer

string or yarn

scissors

HOW?

• Use a hammer and nail to poke a hole in the top and bottom of film containers. (Make several of these ahead of time.)

• Cut a piece of yarn 24" (60 cm) long and thread it through the top and bottom of the film containers. Tie knots in the ends to make a necklace.

• When a child loses a tooth at school, place their tooth in the film container, and let them wear it around their neck until they go home.

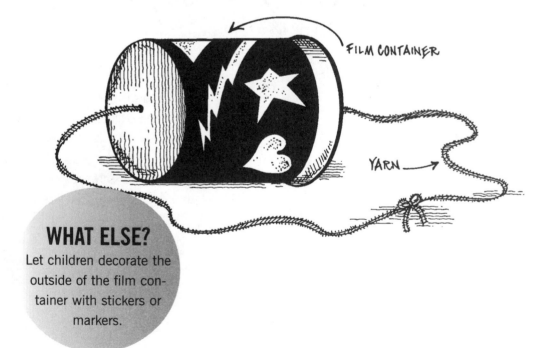

FILM CONTAINER

YARN →

WHAT ELSE?

Let children decorate the outside of the film container with stickers or markers.

Home for Lost Crayons and Pencils

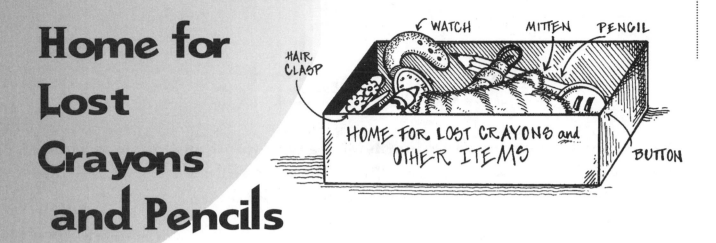

Use this technique for lost and found articles in the classroom.

HOW?
- Cover the shoebox with construction paper and write "Home for Lost Crayons and Other Items" on the side.

- Show it to the children, and explain that they should put crayons, pencils, or other things they find in the box. Place the box on a prominent shelf.

- If children come to you looking for lost articles, remind them to check the box.

WHAT?
shoebox

construction paper

scissors

tape, glue

markers

WHAT ELSE?
Use a larger box or basket for clothing, lunch boxes, toys, and other items. Anytime you find something misplaced, put it in the box so children will learn to accept the responsibility of caring for their materials.

Water Breaks

The brain is composed primarily of water and needs to be replenished every hour with water. Many times if children appear sleepy or inattentive, they just need a drink of water to perk them up.

WHAT?

individual sports bottle, water fountain, or filtered water

HOW?

• Explain to the children that their brains are like sponges. They need water to "freshen" up every hour.

• Model drinking water and exclaim, "Oh, water just perks me up and makes me feel better."

• Encourage the children to take a "water break" every hour on the hour.

WHAT ELSE?

Ask children to bring a sports bottle full of water from home every day when they come to school. If they keep it in their desk or cubby, they can get a quick "sip" when needed.

Tennis Ball Noise Mufflers

This trick with old tennis balls will eliminate noise and scratches on the floor.

HOW?

- Cut slits halfway through the tennis balls. (You will need four balls for each chair.)

- Squeeze the opening, then insert the balls on the bottom of each leg of the chair.

- When children slide the chairs around, the tennis balls will muffle the sound.

WHAT?

old tennis balls

utility knife (teacher only)

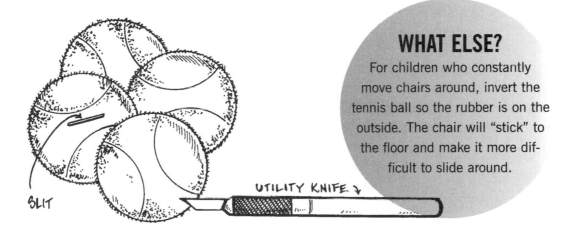

SLIT

UTILITY KNIFE

WHAT ELSE?

For children who constantly move chairs around, invert the tennis ball so the rubber is on the outside. The chair will "stick" to the floor and make it more difficult to slide around.

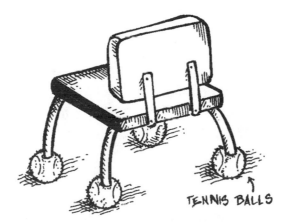

TENNIS BALLS

Rule Book

Empower children and gain their cooperation by allowing them to develop their own classroom rules.

WHAT?

paper

markers

crayons

construction paper

hole punch

book rings

HOW?

• Lead a discussion with the children about rules. What are rules? Why do we have rules? What happens when people don't obey rules? What are some rules that you have in your home? What rules do adults have?

• Explain that you would like them to help you make a book of rules for the classroom so everybody can be safe and have more fun.

• Give each child a piece of paper and ask each child to think of a rule that he thinks is important. Next, ask him to draw a picture of it.

• Go around the room and write sentences about the rules as the children dictate them. (Older children can write their own sentences.)

• Put the children's papers together between a sheet of construction paper, punch holes on the left, and attach with book rings.

• Write "Our Class Rules" on the cover and read over the book with the children. Hang the book in a prominent place in the room, then refer to it when needed. For example, if a child leaves a mess, show him the page in the book that says, "Pick up toys" and remind him that it is a rule. Ask the child what he can do about it, and then follow through.

WHAT ELSE?

Make a separate book for playground rules.

When children are disruptive, take the book down and review the rules. Ask for the children's input on how to enforce the rules.

Pick Me

It's important to children that you are "fair." This procedure will ensure every child gets a turn, and they will appreciate your fairness.

HOW?

• Cover the outside of each can with paper. On one can write "Pick Me." On the other can write "We Had a Turn."

• Let each child decorate a stick by writing his or her name and drawing a face on it. Put all the sticks in the can marked "Pick Me."

• Explain that when you have a special job to be done, you will chose a stick from the can. After they've had a turn, you will put their stick in the other can that says, "We Had a Turn."

• Continue choosing children until everyone has had a turn. You can then return all the sticks to the "Pick Me" can and begin again.

WHAT?

2 empty cans or cups

construction paper

tape

fine-tip markers

large craft sticks

Partner Picks

Use this trick to pair children randomly for games or other partner activities.

WHAT?

large craft sticks

variety of stickers (in pairs)

can

glue

markers

construction paper

WHAT ELSE?

Use seasonal stickers on craft sticks and vary through the year.

For cooperative groups involving four children, cut old postcards or greeting cards into fourths. Pass out the pieces to the children and challenge them to find the matching pieces to make a puzzle. When they get the puzzle together, they'll have their cooperative group.

HOW?

• You will need as many craft sticks as there are children in your classroom. Select two of each sticker and glue them to the bottom of each pair of sticks.

• Cover the can with construction paper and write "Partner Picks" on it. (Use extra stickers to decorate the can.)

• Place the craft sticks with the stickers down in the bottom in the can. Tell the children that when you pass around the can and they should each choose a stick.

• When everyone has a stick, have the children get up and try to find the person with the sticker that matches theirs. That person will then be their partner for the specified activity.

• Listed below are a few projects that partners can enjoy:

Read a book together
Write together
Play in a learning center
Talk or solve a problem

Draw a picture or do an art project
Play a game
Work on a project

STICKS WITH STICKER (AT THE BOTTOM)

CAN COVERED WITH CONSTRUCTION PAPER

Partner Picks

STICKERS

STICKER

Celebrations

These celebrations can be used to focus children's attention, encourage positive behavior, or lift spirits!

HOW?

- Teach your children the following cheers, chants, and movements, then use them during the day to build community, encourage children, or indicate a change in activities.

Firecracker—Put your hands together in front of you. Make a hissing sound as you slowly move them above your head, clap, then extend your arms and wiggle your fingers as you say, "Ahhhh!"

WOW!—Hold up the three middle fingers on each hand. Open your mouth to make the "o" and place the "w" formed by each hand on either side of your mouth.

The Stomp—Begin slowly stomping your foot and clapping this pattern. "Stomp, stomp, clap; stomp, stomp, clap; stomp, stomp, clap" as you chant, "We think we are special." Next, insert each child's name in the chant: "We think Tony is special. We think Lani is special," etc.

Two Thumbs Up—Extend arms in front of you with thumbs up. Say, "Two thumbs up and give it some steam" as you pull your elbows back and make a hissing sound.

Standing Ovation—Stand up and make a circle or "O" above your head.

Silent Cheer—Put arms in the air, wiggle fingers, open mouth, and pretend to yell. (Tell the children they can make as much noise as they want, as long as you don't hear them.)

Opera Applause—Clap with index fingers.

Clam Applause—Make pincers with fingers and open and shut.

Seal of Approval—Extend arms stiffly in front of you and make barking noises as you clap hands.

Penguin Applause—Put hands by your side, bend hands so they are pointed out, and flap arms.

WHAT?

no materials needed

FIRECRACKER

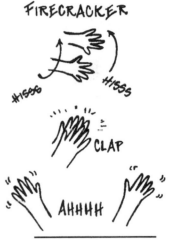

WOW

THE STOMP

2-4-6-8 Cheer—Clap hands as you go around the room and insert each child's name in this chant, "2-4-6-8, We think Kevin is great!"

Drum Roll—Pretend the floor or table is a drum and tap it with your fingers.

Beethoven—Tell the children to pretend to get out their cellos as you demonstrate how you would hold the instrument. Pretend to play as you sing the melody to Beethoven's Fifth Symphony and say, "Da da da daaaa, da da da daaa."

Pat on the Back—Tell the children to pat themselves on the back for doing such a good job.

Cowboy—Put your finger in the air and twirl it around as you say, "Yee haw!"

Parrot—Put your hands under your armpits to make wings. Lift your elbows as you squawk, "Aaak, you did a good job! Aaak, you did a good job!

PENGUIN APPLAUSE   2-4-6-8 CHEER   TWO THUMBS UP

SEAL OF APPROVAL   DRUM ROLL   STANDING OVATION

BEETHOVEN   OPERA APPLAUSE

CLAM APPLAUSE

Help Wanted

This book will encourage children to think of the many different ways people can be talented. It will also nurture group cohesiveness and interdependence.

HOW?

- Tear the front and back cover off old yellow pages.

- Make different pages to go in the book that represent the different multiple intelligences. You might write the following at the top of the pages:

  We can draw well.
  We like math.
  We can spell well.
  We are good at sports.
  We can tie shoes.
  We are good readers.

  We can make you happy.
  We like to make friends.
  We like to clean.
  We can help you solve problems.
  We like to sing.

- Place the pages in between the covers of the phone book, punch holes, and attach with the book rings. Write "(Teacher's Name) Classroom Yellow Pages."

- Introduce the book to the class by telling them some of the things you can do well, as well as some of the areas you are weak in. Ask the children to share things they are good at and things they need to work on.

- Show them the book and explain how people use the yellow pages to find "help" when they need it. Explain that in the same way, they can use the book to get "help" from their classmates when they need help.

- Ask the children to dictate or sign their names on the pages they think they are good at. Encourage them to sign several different pages.

- When a child needs help, refer them to the Classroom Yellow Pages.

WHAT?

old yellow pages

paper

markers

hole punch

2 book rings

HINT!
Use picture clues for the younger children.

We can draw well.

Jim   Kate

HOLES FOR BOOK RINGS

We like to sing

Sara
Judy

Parent Concerns

If parents need to tell you something while you are busy with the children, this book may be the trick you need.

WHAT?

notebook

pen

HOW?

• Write "Parent Concerns" on the front of the notebook.

• Tape a statement similar to the one below on the notebook:

Dear Parents:

I realize there will be times in the school day when you have important things you want to discuss with me. However, when the children are in the room, they need and deserve my undivided attention. Therefore, please write your problem or question in this notebook. Leave a phone number where I can get in touch with you today or this evening. As soon as I get a break, I will try to get back to you with an answer.

Thanks for your cooperation.

• Place the notebook with an attached pen near your classroom door.

• If a parent comes in, hand them the notebook and continue working with the children. Nod or give them a nonverbal signal when they are finished.

Red and Green

Green means "go" and "red" means stop—a unique way to manage your classroom with these color indicators.

HOW?

- Each child will need to decorate his or her own plastic lid. They should cover one side with green construction paper, and the other side with red.

- Ask the children what the colors represent on the traffic light.

- Explain that they can use the same colors to indicate if they are on a "go" or if they need you to "stop" and help them.

- As they work on independent activities, tell them to place their lid next to them with the appropriate color up. You will be able to quickly walk around the room and see who needs extra help.

WHAT?

plastic lids

scissors

glue

red and green construction paper

WHAT ELSE?

Red and green plastic cups can be used in a similar manner. They simply place the red cup on top to signal if they need help, or the green cup if they are doing fine.

The teacher can use similar color indicators to let the children know if it's time to get quiet (red) or if they are ready to go (green).

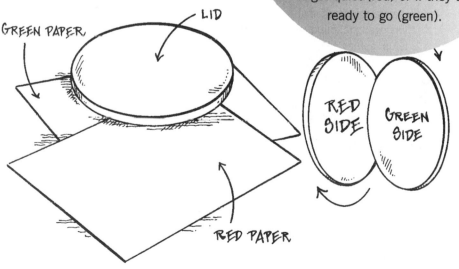

Think Buddies

When there is not time to listen to each child respond orally, use Think Buddies to give them the opportunity to verbalize their thoughts and discuss information.

WHAT?

no materials needed

HOW?

• Ask the children to turn to the person sitting next to them and be Think Buddies.

• Use these partners in situations similar to those below:

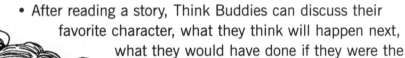

  • After reading a story, Think Buddies can discuss their favorite character, what they think will happen next, what they would have done if they were the ____, where the story occurred, what the problem was and what a solution might be, and so forth.

  • When you teach a concept lesson, Think Buddies can explain what they learned to each other.

  • To review what children did at center time, have them talk about their activities with a friend.

• At the end of the day, use Think Buddies for the children to discuss what they liked best at school or something new they learned.

• Use Think Buddies to solve problem classroom situations. For example, "Friends are forgetting to clean up the art center. What do you think we can do about it?"

• Encourage the Think Buddies to summarize a learning experience.

Good-Bye Book

Moving during the school year can be traumatic for the child leaving, as well as for their classmates. This activity is a positive way to say farewell and send children off with positive thoughts.

HOW?

• Pass out a plain sheet of paper to each child.

• Explain to the children that their friend, (child's name), is moving and you'd like their help in making a book so the child will remember the class.

• Ask each child to draw a picture and write or dictate a sentence about what they like about the friend that is moving. The teacher should draw a picture as well.

• The child who is moving decorates the construction paper cover, or takes a photograph of the class and glues it on the front.

• Place construction paper on top of the pictures the children have made, punch holes through all the pieces of paper, and tie together with yarn.

WHAT?

plain paper

markers, crayons

construction paper

hole punch

yarn

WHAT ELSE?

When a child moves, ask the children to brainstorm ways they can keep in touch with someone who doesn't live near them. For example, they could call, fax pictures, write letters, and so on.

If a child is moving, ask the parents to send a disposable camera for their child to take pictures of the school and their friends.

CHAPTER 9

End of the Day

Send children home with a song in their heart
using these parting tunes and rituals.
The end of the day is also the perfect opportunity
to review daily activities and have children
recall what they learned or enjoyed.

Yee Haw, Good-Bye!

Create group cohesiveness and positive feelings about school with this ritual song.

WHAT?

no materials needed

HOW?

- Begin clapping your hands as you sing or chant:

Yee Haw, Good-Bye! (Tune: "She'll Be Comin' 'Round the Mountain")

It is time to say "good-bye" to all my friends. (clap hands)
It is time to say "good-bye" to all my friends.
It is time to say "good-bye,"
Give a smile and wink your eye. (smile and wink eye)
It is time to say "good-bye" to all my friends.
Yee haw! (cheer with fist in the air)

WHAT ELSE?

Wave your hand as you sing or chant this farewell song:

We Say Good-Bye
(Tune: "The Farmer in the Dell")

We say good-bye like this. (wave)
We say good-bye like this.
We clap our hands (clap hands)
For all our friends,
And say good-bye like this.
(wave)

On Our Way Home

Use this song to prepare children to leave at the end of the day.

HOW?

• Clap your hands or slap your thighs to gain children's attention before you sing this song.

On Our Way (Tune: "She'll Be Comin' 'Round the Mountain")
We'll be going home in a bus.
Beep! Beep!
We'll be going home in a bus.
Beep! Beep!
We'll be going home,
We'll be going home,
We'll be going home in a bus.
Beep! Beep!

• Have children tell you how they will get home, then change the words of the song:

We'll be going home in our van. Rmm! Rmm!...
We'll be going home in our car. Honk! Honk!...
We'll be going home on our feet. Walk! Walk!...

WHAT?

no materials needed

WHAT ELSE?

Ask children to think of other ways to travel, then make up verses, such as:
We'll be going downtown on the train. Choo! Choo!
We'll be going to grandma's on a jet. Rrrr! Rrrr!

What Did You Do in School?

Use this chant to bring closure and review what the children did during the day.

WHAT?

no materials needed

HOW?

- Before children go home at the end of the day, ask them to think of something they did that they enjoyed.

- Tell them when they hear their name, they can tell you what they liked best.

- Go around the room inserting each child's name in this chant:

  Hey, (child's name)!
  What do you say?
  What did you do
  In school today?

WHAT ELSE?

Write children's responses on a language experience chart.

Take a photograph of each child engaged in their favorite activity. Write the chant and what they like to do under their picture. Put the pages together to make a class book called, "What Do We Do in School?" Let children have turns taking the book home and sharing it with their families.

HEY MARK!
WHAT DO YOU SAY?
WHAT DID YOU DO
IN SCHOOL TODAY?

I MADE A CLAY
SNAKE!

Recall Roundup

Brain research emphasizes the importance of having children recall information. This technique is a perfect way to end your day as you encourage children to review what they have learned.

HOW?

• Sit in a circle.

• Ask the children to think of something new they learned at school that day and to share it with the group when you toss them the ball.

• That child may either toss the ball back to you, or may toss it to a friend.

• Continue until each child has had a turn.

WHAT?

beanbag or sponge ball

HINT!

Here's an easy way to make a beanbag. Put a cup of dried beans in the toe of an old sock. Wrap a rubber band around the toe to form a ball. Pull the cuff of the sock over the beans.

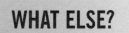

BEANBAGS MADE OUT OF OLD SOCKS

SPONGE BALL

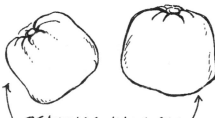

WHAT ELSE?

Ask the children to share what they liked most at school that day when you toss them the ball.

Review particular concepts you are working on with Recall Roundup. For example, you could ask children to name a farm animal, think of something that starts with the "P" sound, name an object that is shaped like a triangle, tell a sign of spring, and so on.

Paper House Recall

This drawing activity is another excellent way to help children recall learning experiences.

WHAT?	HOW?
paper	• Fold the top corners of the paper down to the middle, as illustrated.
crayons	• Fold up the bottom so it looks like a house.
markers	• Have children "open" their house and draw what they did at school.
pencils	• Tell the children to take their houses home and tell their families about their day at school.

WHAT ELSE?

Have children write or dictate a sentence to go along with their picture.

Use houses to have children illustrate favorite stories, such as "Goldilocks," "Three Little Pigs," "Little Red Riding Hood," or "The Gingerbread Man."

←HOUSE

Memory Book

A Memory Book is another way for children to recall information and develop reading and writing skills.

HOW?

- Ask the children to describe what a "memory" is and to share different memories that they have.

- Tell them they will each get to make their own Memory Book in which they can draw pictures and write about special things that happen to them at school that they want to remember.

- Demonstrate how to make a memory book, then let the children each make their own.

- Count out 20 pieces of plain white paper. Fold the construction paper in half and insert the white paper. Staple in place.

- Encourage the children to write their names on their books and decorate the cover with crayons, markers, or other art media.

- Set aside a few minutes before children leave each day so they can draw pictures in their books. Encourage the children to "write" or be available to take dictation for them.

WHAT?

white paper 8 ½" x 11" (21.25 cm x 27.5 cm)

construction paper 12" x 18" (30 cm x 45 cm)

stapler

pencils, pens, crayons, markers

WHAT ELSE?

Provide children with a date stamp so they can date their pages.

Make new Memory Books each month. Ask parents to send in a spiral ring notebook and use these for memory books. Store Memory Books in the writing center so children have access to them during the day.

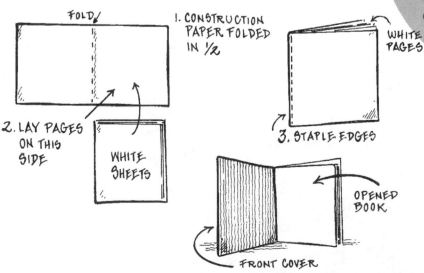

FOLD

I. CONSTRUCTION PAPER FOLDED IN ½

2. LAY PAGES ON THIS SIDE

WHITE SHEETS

WHITE PAGES

3. STAPLE EDGES

OPENED BOOK

FRONT COVER

Left at Home and Bring Right Back

Use this folder daily to develop responsibility in children and establish routine communication with parents.

WHAT?

pocket folders

markers, crayons

paper

scissors

glue

HOW?

- Let the children decorate the cover of their file folders with their names and drawings.

- Help the children trace around their hands on construction paper and cut them out.

- Glue the left hands to the left pockets of the folders and write, "**Left** at home."

- Glue the right hands to the right pockets and write, "Bring **right** back."

- Use this folder to transport things that need to be sent home with the child, such as a newsletter, on the left side, and things that need to be returned, such as a field trip permission, on the right side.

- Explain to parents at a parent meeting or in a newsletter how you will use this folder and that they should check it each day.

- Parents can also use it to send notes into school.

WHAT ELSE?

Tape a recloseable plastic bag to the right folder to hold lunch money.

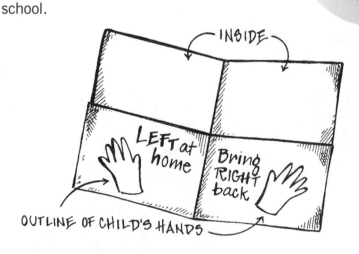

OUTLINE OF CHILD'S HANDS

INSIDE

LEFT at home

Bring RIGHT back

Special Delivery

Special Delivery is a guaranteed way to get notes and messages home to parents.

HOW?

- Cover the canister with construction paper and write "Special Delivery" on it.

- Let the children decorate the can with markers or stickers. (For best results, cover with clear contact paper or a self-laminating sheet.)

- When you have a special note to send home with a child, put it in the can and explain to the child that it's a "special delivery" for parents.

- Tell her she has an important job: to give the note to her parents and bring back the empty can the next day.

WHAT?

potato chip canister

construction paper

tape, glue

markers

POTATO CHIP CANISTER

SPECIAL DELIVERY

WHAT ELSE?

Ask each child to bring in an empty food canister. Let them decorate it with wallpaper and other art scraps. Make sure they put their name on the can. Use the can daily for them to take home their projects and papers.

Yearbook

A class yearbook is a meaningful way for children to recall past experiences and build positive memories about school.

WHAT?

camera

film

photo album

HINT!

You might want to ask each family to donate a roll of film or a disposable camera at the beginning of the school year.

HOW?

- Take pictures of the children as they enter the classroom the first day of school.

- Put children's pictures in the photo album, along with a short description about them.

- You might have them complete sentences similar to those below:

    My name is _____.
    My eyes are _____.
    My favorite color is _____.
    My favorite food is _____.
    I am special because _____.

- As you go through the school year, take pictures of special events, such as field trips, class parties, guests, cooking experiences, projects, etc.

- Add photos to the album along with captions.

- Use the Yearbook frequently to build self-esteem, recall good times, and encourage children to describe past experiences.

WHAT ELSE?

This is an excellent book for your classroom library. Children will enjoy looking at it individually or with a friend.

Let one child take the book home each evening to share with her family.

Encourage parents to browse through the book when they come in for parent conferences.

LEARNING ABOUT COLORS

SEPT.

FINISHED ART WORK

HALLOWEEN COSTUME

MAKING TURKEY PLACE CARDS

Timeline

This project will enable children to revisit classroom experiences and recall information.

HOW?

- Tape a long strip of adding-machine paper to a wall in the classroom.

- Explain to the children that you will use it to help them remember all the exciting things that happen in their classroom that year.

- Write the date of the first day of school. Take a photograph of the children or ask a child to draw a picture about that first day.

- Add different significant events, such as children's birthdays, field trips, themes, and other special memories. Date these and document with photographs or children's drawings.

- Frequently refer to the timeline to refresh children's memories or revisit a past event.

WHAT?

adding-machine paper

tape

markers, crayons

photographs

WHAT ELSE?

This can be used to track the whole school year, or just one month.

Let children make timelines of their lives.

September 6 September 10 September 24 October 2 October 17

Index